Miss Chev

Philippa Church

Research and Collaboration: Rosie Sandler

Foreword

My initial conversation with Philippa Church was gently but insistently interrupted by Lily, her velvet nosed golden Labrador. Although who owned whom was a matter for conjecture, the large, floppy friendly Labrador is obviously Philippa's prized possession, showering devotion and hot panting breath in equal proportions.

 Since her childhood time of days filled with the excitements of reading 'The Secret Garden,' Philippa has dreamed of owning acres of bookshelves filled with the stories of ancient books. It is an intense and satisfying hobby in that she trawls the second-hand book stores searching for books that tell of the fulfilment of a true family life. Although she has many happy memories of working within the Fashion Store industry she has found an intense and enervating interest researching the letters that she found in a folder at her grandmother's family house. Trawling family archives and the Victoria and Albert Museum she has produced a story based upon facts that illustrate the realities of the early Twentieth Century and the involvements of real people and their love for each other.

Philippa has asked that it be well understood that whilst this story is based upon real events and happenings of the time, the characters portrayed may well be illustrative of individuals who played a part in the structure(s) of events but in no way should be taken as an accurate description of people or family members, living or dead. The story is based upon family archival remains and is the product of Philippa's view of how events may well have happened...

Terry G-F ....editor 2016

BLACKHEATH DAWN
Blackheath Dawn Publishing

Hafren House, Blackheath, Wenhaston. Suffolk IP199HB
Email: enquiries.blackheathdawn@gmail.com

© Philippa Church 2016

Miss Chevrolet

ISBN 978-1-911368-02-1

Miss Chevrolet is a fictional novel, based upon fact. As such it reflects the author's experiences over time. Some names and characters have been added or altered to ensure pertinent dialogue and to fit within the likely time frames.

For more information on Philippa Church

Enquiries.Blackheathdawn@gmail.com

Acknowledgements

I would like to thank all of my friends for constant inspiration and support. It has been a long journey but their help was invaluable..

Thank you to Vauxhall Archives for putting up with my questions and coming back with all the relevant information.

Thank you to Terry Gilbert-Fellows, my editor/proof reader, who stuck by me; his loyal encouragement kept me working with the story. I love the front cover with Mary Gundry's painting. When I asked Mary Gundry for a watercolour painting of a car and an attractive woman, this wonderful artist came up with a perfect representation that inspired me to strive to produce a story that might hopefully approach the quality of her talent.

Thank you to Rosie Sandler for her help, friendliness and her collaboration and research of the era in which the story is mainly set.

A special thank you to my mothers' garden for the beautiful flowers, so that I could paint watercolours for my greeting cards.

Philippa Church 2016

No way was that folder to go with the rest of the attic contents; I carefully hid it beneath my bed for later scrutiny- I just knew that it would prove to be important........

...........With tears in my eyes I waved goodbye to the furniture and the last of my family. I was to remain in the house until the new owners took possession. I returned to the kitchen table with my lovely dog. Tea in hand, I excitedly unclipped the leather folder, drew down the zip and was immediately transported backwards in time........

.... Alice my beautiful grandmother describing her clothes, her family and travel to Egypt to be married to my Grandfather. Love letters, yes, but so much more; they told of a life that existed, a passion that moved through time and I was able to experience and relate their happiness and endearing love ....

Prologue

Fleur stood watching the last car head off slowly along the long, curved driveway. Her aunt waved and blew kisses from the passenger's seat; Fleur blew a kiss back. She took a deep breath in the balmy evening air, enjoying the strong, sweet scent of the rambling roses and honeysuckle that scrambled over the old yew hedges. Her mother had loved those roses – she had preferred them to the upright tea roses, which she described as 'uptight' and 'strait-laced': she had liked her garden to reflect its countryside setting. Fleur blinked back a tear as the flowers' perfume mingled with her memories of her mother. It was all still too raw.

Her uncle's Vauxhall Vectra disappeared around the bend. It was many years since Uncle Ralph's father – Fleur's grandfather – had been involved with General Motors but her uncle was still fiercely loyal to the company:

'GM is in my blood,' he'd say when questioned about his choice. 'I don't need some show-off car, which just announces to the world that the driver is rich and vain.'

As always, thoughts of cars reminded Fleur of the old Chevrolet, still housed in the garage. No one had driven that beautiful girl for a while, and she hid beneath her black cover like a widow beneath her veil.

One day soon I'll get you out, Fleur vowed silently to the car, and you and I will go for a spin in the little country lanes, with your hood down and the wind in my hair. Your engine will be able to sing again.

Fleur turned back to the house with a sigh. While all the family had been here at Wisteria Cottage, she had found it easy to distract herself. They had divided up possessions, and she had watched vans pull up, and burly removal men fill them with huge armoires, dressers, bedside tables and King Louis IV chairs, under the direction of various family members. After all, there was so much furniture in the old house, and she wouldn't need a lot of it, living here alone until the sale went through.

They'd had none of the squabbles she'd heard about: awful rows, as one family member insisted he or she had more right than another to some valuable heirloom. She even knew of one brother and sister in the village who hadn't spoken to one another since their great-uncle had died, and the sister had seized the rocking-chair which the brother had been coveting.

But there'd been nothing like that among Fleur's relatives. She felt pride spread through her, warming her, as she acknowledged the respect with which they had all treated this house and its contents. And it had been good to watch her mother's well-loved pieces move on, and to know they would be treasured anew. She had made plans already to visit the rest of my family, and there would be welcome sights there – familiar pieces of furniture, awaiting her like old friends.

And she still had her own piece of treasure awaiting her, on the kitchen table…

Hattie the dog followed Fleur down to the kitchen, where she boiled the kettle for tea. As she took her mug over to the table and sat down, Hattie came over, tail wagging forlornly, and sat at Fleur's feet, with her head in her lap.

'You miss her too, girl, don't you?' said Fleur. The adorable, if slightly overweight, sandy-coloured Labrador gazed up into her eyes with a puzzled expression. 'I'm sorry, Hattie-girl – she's not coming back.'

A few tears leaked from Fleur's eyes. She seemed to have no control over her eyes at the moment, and they would often start to cry without warning and certainly without any apparent intention of stopping. Hattie licked her hand in empathy.

In front of Fleur on the table lay the one thing that she'd been looking forward to, through all the aftermath of losing her mother. It was her sister Tilly who'd found it when she and Fleur were on loft-clearing duty. Tilly had uncovered a box stuffed full of photograph albums, which she had riffled through. At the bottom, she found a leather folder, which she handed to Fleur, who took it eagerly.

'But, don't you want to see what's inside it?' Fleur asked.

Tilly shrugged. 'Mummy showed me once: it's full of letters. We don't have time to go through them at the moment.'

'Letters?' Fleur held the folder with both hands and drew it to her chest like a talisman that might protect her from cold reality. She was so tired of sorting and sifting and unpacking and re-packing… She imagined sitting down on one of the beams in that dusty attic space, and losing herself in the world of whoever had written them. 'Can we take a look?'

Tilly gestured to the stacks of boxes in the loft, 'We've got all of this to sort through yet. Why don't you go through the folder later, and let me know if you find anything interesting?'

At lunchtime, Fleur had carried various boxes down to the landing and then stashed the folder under her bed, where it wouldn't get swept up by mistake in the house-clearing frenzy. Her room was the one place that no one was allowed to enter: she had to be able to retreat when it all became too much.

Now, she stroked the outside of the folder, as if it were a living creature whose trust she needed to gain.

'This is it, Hattie,' she whispered to the dog, who had her eyes half-closed in sleepiness. Her tail moved slowly along the floor at the sound of Fleur's voice.

Fleur hesitated a moment longer, her fingers shaking. She took a sip of her tea.

At last, she undid the strap and opened the folder.

Inside, there were many letters and postcards. Fleur recognised her grandmother Alice's writing, and her heart seemed to seize for a moment as if squeezed in a tight fist. Even after all this time, the pain of loss was intense, and often caught her off-guard – especially since her mother's recent passing.

Her grandmother had died five years earlier, but Fleur still missed her. She had been such a force – a whirlwind of tall, slender glamour, elegance and sharp wit. Even in her eighties, she still wore beautiful, tailored clothes, with glossy pointed shoes and immaculate make-up. She was the most stylish woman Fleur had ever known. She pictured her grandmother's clothes, which until this week had hung in three beautiful mahogany wardrobes here at her mother's. When Fleur was younger, Grandma Alice used to let her dress up in those fabulous dresses, which had labels hand-stitched inside, boasting names like BIBA and Chanel. They would laugh together as Fleur placed her tiny feet into pointed snakeskin shoes and attempted to walk in the heels, trailing swathes of oversize skirt fabric like a wedding train.

Now, though, Fleur's older brother had taken those wardrobes and decanted their contents into a large trunk. She must make sure she took care of the clothes before moths could get in and destroy them. She wondered whether the Victoria & Albert Museum might be interested in some of the more elaborate pieces; there was a dress stitched with tiny sequins, forming an elaborate pattern in black and silver, and another that was a wonderful, shimmering golden sheath from the nineteen-twenties. And as for the hats… There was a whole collection of them, from bell-shape cloches to flirty little toques, Jackie O-style pillboxes, and nineteen-seventies' wide-brim sunhats. The latter were back in fashion, and Fleur thought she might try one or two, to see if they suited her. She made a mental note to have a hat-modelling session when she was feeling a little more upbeat. Perhaps Tilly might like to come over and join her: they could try on some of the clothes, as well. Those wonderful snakeskin shoes might actually fit her, after all this time.

She waited for her eyes to clear of tears, and then she turned her gaze to the top letter in the folder. As she read, she felt as if she was travelling back to 1924, to when her grandmother was young. Absorbed in this previous era, she forgot that she was sitting alone in a country house with a dog. Instead, she became a sophisticated woman-of-the-world, about to embark on the adventure of a lifetime. She was Alice, and she was going to Egypt.

Chapter One

22 Beaumont Street

London

1 May, 1928

My Dear Henry,

Many thanks for your last letter, which I selfishly kept to myself and read three times, before finally allowing Mother to see it! It is always such a joy to hear about your life in Egypt and to imagine myself there, by your side. I miss you terribly, of course. In fact, despite all of your protestations to the contrary, I am quite sure that I miss you more than you can possibly miss me, because you sound so busy, with all your business dealings.

I, meanwhile, can do nothing but plan my trousseau and attend Mrs. Florence's musical evenings... Don't I sound provincial, compared with your cosmopolitan dinner parties? I do hope you won't be disappointed in me, by the time we finally meet again. Perhaps you will have become accustomed to such sophisticated ladies, that I shall appear almost a country bumpkin in comparison!

Henry, is it very wrong of me to admit that I am, at times, seized by terror at the thought of the journey and the new life before me? What will Egypt be like? Will there be servants who don't even speak my language? What if the heat is too intense for me, with my pale, English complexion?

Mother would reprimand me if she knew I was troubling you with what she considers being purely trivial concerns. Father, meanwhile, would probably laugh and pat my head – as if I were one of his dogs, caught performing an amusing trick. You are the only person who listens to me. I find it hard to believe that we really will be united soon, and for the rest of our lives. I must be the luckiest woman alive.

Do write again soon, with more details about the house. I have been looking through Father's picture books on Egypt, but none of them shows a villa with a veranda such as you describe. The porch swing sounds simply delightful! Are the mosquitoes really so troublesome, though, that one must have nets strung against them, across all the doors and windows?

A few days ago, I was browsing through a recent issue of "Vogue" magazine, and one of the writers suggested one must even wear a hat with a veil when visiting any of the African countries. Can this really be entirely necessary, do you think? Mother has ordered several such hats to be made up especially – but I hate the idea of having to be so covered-up. Perhaps these frightful insects are really a problem only during the damp season. Meanwhile, I am having Lucy pack an enormous trunk, with all of the medicines suggested by Doctor Stanway. If he is to be believed, I need upon arrival take only one step from the ship, to be assailed by at least a dozen of the deadliest plagues. I find it hard to keep a straight face when the Doctor's messenger boy arrives at the house with the latest list of 'necessities', but Mother says it is, 'better to be safe than sorry', and I suppose she is right.

How are you getting on, with fixing up your new offices? Have you managed to find someone with sufficient experience, to be your right-hand man? I do wish I could picture your office and all the men working in it, sorting the *various parts and preparing them for transportation. Is it very noisy?*

Oh: Mother says I must ask you if you have a preference as to white or pink flowers for the reception. She would like to have everything white on the tables (she believes this colour scheme would be more 'elegant' and 'tasteful'), but I think a splash of pink would be rather nice, don't you?

I am striking off the days on my calendar, Henry, until my parents and I will set sail. How excited and scared I am, in almost equal measure!

Write soon, my darling, write soon, write soon,

Your loving fiancée,

Alice

***

1927

Henry straightened his tie as he walked through the revolving door of the Harpenden Motor Company headquarters in Luton. The place was huge: a testament to Harpenden's success in this relatively new marketplace. He dusted the rain off his coat and gave his trilby a shake over the door mat before heading over to the desk.

The guard on the reception desk doffed his cap. He was a broad, red-faced man, with a pleasant expression.

'Good day, Sir. May I ask who you're visiting today?'

'The Director of Export Sales, Mr. Faraday.'

'And your name?'

'Henry Pemberton. I have an interview.'

'An interview, 'eh? I'll just ring up to Mr. Faraday's secretary…' He picked up the phone and spoke into the receiver. 'Frieda? I've got a Mr. Pemberton here, for Mr. Faraday. Right, will do.' He replaced the receiver. 'Mr. Faraday would like you to go straight up to his office, Sir. He's on the third floor, but Sylvio in the lift will put you right. I'll take your hat and coat, shall I, sir?'

He relieved Henry of these items, before escorting him to the lift, where he spoke briefly to the lift man: 'See Mr. Pemberton here gets to Frieda on the third, will you, Sylvio?'

The lift man saluted smartly and nodded to Henry, who walked inside.

'Well, best of luck to you, Mr. Pemberton,' said the reception guard.

'Thank you. May I ask your name?'

'George, Sir. Like our good King himself.'

The lift doors closed, and Henry shut his eyes. As a child, he had loved the movement of lifts – the sense of being outside space, of travelling almost through time itself – but now, as an adult, he found the movement could make him queasy: a curious state of affairs for a man who loved movement generally, and was never happier than when behind the wheel of a car. Fortunately, the journey to the third floor was soon over, and, as George had promised, he was greeted at once by Frieda. She was a small, round woman, who gave off a reassuring, motherly air. He followed her bustling form down a long corridor, to a large office at the end, where the air was so thick with cigar smoke, it took Henry a moment to make out the figure within. A bald, stocky man sat behind a mahogany desk which was heaped with papers. He resembled an educated dragon, breathing fire from his cigar while scouring documents. He looked up from the paperwork he was perusing as the two of them entered.

'Mr. Faraday,' said Frieda, 'I have Mr. Pemberton here, for his eleven o'clock interview.'

'Very good, Frieda. Hold my calls, would you?'

'Yes, Sir.'

As Frieda left the room, Henry moved to approach his interviewer. However, he stopped abruptly when his eye was caught by the photograph of a familiar vehicle, on one of the wood-panelled walls. Forgetting where he was, he moved over for a closer look.

'You like her?' asked Mr. Faraday, after a moment.

Henry snapped out of his trance. 'I'm sorry, Sir, but it's "Babs" – the car that broke the land speed record back in April…' He gestured to the sleek silhouette of the racing car in the frame.

'That's right: 171 miles per hour.'

'Parry-Thomas is my hero.'

The director smiled. 'I think he's every man's hero. Did you know we made the carburettor for "Babs" here at Harpenden?'

'Now you mention it, I think I did read that somewhere…'

'I've heard Campbell is planning a new challenge early next year, in his latest model of "Blue Bird",' said Faraday.

'Well, if anyone can do it, it's Campbell.'

'My thoughts entirely… Now, take a seat, won't you? You're making me nervous.'

Henry sat down quickly, in one of the three elegant, curve-back chairs lined up facing the large desk. 'I'm sorry, Sir – I got distracted by that photograph of "Babs".'

'Well, if it's beautiful cars you're into, Mr. Pemberton, you've come to the right place.' He glanced down at Henry's job application on the desk. 'Henry, is it? You can call me Johnny. Cigar?'

Henry accepted the proffered cigar. Really, he would have preferred to abstain, but he felt Faraday wasn't the type to take No for an answer. Not until one had secured a job with him, at least.

As if reading his mind, Faraday said, 'So, you want a job?' He sucked on his cigar and blew out a ring of smoke. Henry took a small drag on his own cigar and tried not to choke at the strong, thick fumes. He nodded and waved away some of the smoke with one hand.

'Yes, please. I have experience which I think would tie in perfectly with what you're looking for.'

Faraday gave an indulgent smile. 'And what am I looking for?'

'Someone dynamic, who understands the motor trade and the pressures it's currently under. Someone who is passionate about the Harpenden marque and would love the chance to see it grow and prosper.'

'What do you know about Harpenden?'

'I know the firm was founded in 1919, by Samuel Harper and Benjamin Denver. I know that it started out as a small operation, refurbishing vehicles for the wealthy.'

'And now?'

'Now, it's the first choice for the discerning customer of luxurious, quality vehicles. Harpenden isn't cheap, but it produces beautiful specimens. Since Sharpe and Stephens came over to head up the design side, the cars have become coveted items – never as many produced as there is demand. I also know that the next model, "Queenie" is about to launch – and from what I've heard, she's a real beauty. They say there are already several hundred names on the waiting list.'

Faraday leaned forward. 'You've done your research, all right. So, what do you see in the company's future?'

Henry thought for a moment. 'I see the need to retain the company's image as the truly luxurious option for the lucky few. However, I feel there is space for expansion within that.'

'You do, 'eh? Where do you see that happening?'

'In a smaller vehicle, aimed at the younger market – the sons and daughters of the proud owners of Harpenden's current cars. Something sleek and neat for the young women, with a flashier version for the young men.'

Faraday said nothing. He picked up Henry's cv and read it through.

'Your experience…'

'…is with my father's company. I've been sales director for three years now, and sales and exports have increased exponentially.'

'Very impressive. But you've been working on selling fine cloths, I believe?'

'That's right.'

'So, nothing to do with the motor industry?'

'No, but I have followed it passionately.'

'"Passionately", is it? Passion and enthusiasm are all very well, but can you tell me why you think we should take a chance on you when you have no experience whatsoever in selling cars?'

'A good salesman can sell anything, so long as he believes in it.'

Faraday nodded and wiped away some ash that had fallen on his desk. Without warning, he pushed back his chair and stood up, then strode towards the door. He had a heavy frame, like a bulldog or a rugby player. Henry sat still, unsure what was expected of him.

The director glanced back. 'Well, come on – don't you want to get a drink and celebrate your new position?'

As they took the lift down, Faraday introduced him to Sylvio, the lift attendant.

'This is our new Export Sales Rep, Sylvio. Treat him well.'

'I will, Sir,' said Sylvio, touching his cap deferentially.

As the doors opened, Faraday turned to Henry. 'There's someone I want you to meet before we go for that drink,' he said. He strode out of the lift and towards the revolving exit doors, before stopping mid-stride.

'Oh, George,' he said, addressing the reception guard, 'Can you let Frieda know I've gone out for a bit? And she can tell the other interviewees to go home.'

'Righto, Sir – will do,' said George. He magicked Henry's coat from somewhere and passed it to him.

A young man with gleaming Brilliantined hair was sitting in the waiting area. After hearing this interchange between Faraday and George, he put down the magazine he was browsing and looked forlorn. Henry guessed he was there for the interviews.

Faraday headed out through the door and Henry moved to follow him. George thrust Henry's coat at him and gave him a wink and a thumbs-up.

'Looks like we'll be seeing more of you, Sir,' he said.

'Looks that way,' said Henry, with a grin.

When he got outside, Faraday was already half-way across the courtyard, and Henry had to jog to catch up.

'Just in here,' said Faraday, gesturing to a large, hangar-like building, which Henry guessed was one of the factories.

Inside, the noise was furious. Men in white coats moved around like surgeons, guiding machinery. Long rows of women sat further along, piecing together smaller components. No one spoke: they wouldn't be heard if they did.

Keeping up his fast, loping pace, Faraday approached a winding staircase that led to a mezzanine level above. Henry followed him, marvelling at how such a big man could move so effortlessly: he climbed the staircase as nimbly as a cat. Despite his own regular tennis-playing, Henry was panting by the time he reached the top. He stopped to catch his breath and take in the scene, looking first up at the rafters – still many metres above his head – and then down, at the floor below, where the workers were reduced to miniatures.

'It's a good spot to oversee the whole domain,' said Faraday, close to his ear. Henry nodded.

It was slightly quieter up here. Faraday greeted a couple of men in white coats by clapping them on the shoulders; he bent to explain in Henry's ear: 'Two of our top engineers, Jones and Whittaker.'

Henry shook them each by the hand. Then his gaze was distracted by the beauty of the car on which the engineers were working. It was the much-anticipated Harpenden 'Queenie': long and white, and with a curved bonnet. It was a dream of a car.

'She's really something, isn't she?' said Faraday, following his gaze. 'Come over. You want to sit in her?'

Henry blushed. 'Oh, no – that's all right.'

'Go on – you're not going to harm her, just by sitting in the driving seat.' The two engineers were laughing now, and Henry couldn't resist. He eased himself on to the cream leather seat and took the wheel between his hands. What he'd give, to drive a car like this.

Two hours later, having enjoyed a drink and a bite to eat, Henry and Faraday shook hands back at the Harpenden car park. Henry smiled as he walked to his vehicle; the sun was shining as if it knew good things were coming.

***

Alice stepped out from behind the screen, and the small group of staff gathered around the board table gave a collective gasp.

'It's like molten silver,' said one lady reverentially, gazing at the hat atop Alice's head. Alice recognised her as one of the head buyers, who was prone to sentimentality.

'How does it feel to wear?' asked Billy Francis, who ran the Debonair hat company's flagship store in Bond Street.

'Well, it would be all right, except it has got something sharp inside it.' Alice put a hand up to the offending area.

Her mother got up from her chair and walked over to her. 'Take it off, and let me have a look.' Alice removed the hat and passed it to her mother, who took it with both hands and turned it upside-down, peering inside.

'A pin!' her mother exclaimed. 'How many times have I told them in the workshop to check and check again?' She reached in and removed the offending object, before handing the hat back to her daughter.

'Try it on now, Alice, and let us know if it feels all right.'

Alice pulled the cloche back on. It wasn't really her style – sitting a little lower than she liked, and being rather too ornate. Alice preferred her hats neater and quirkier: an unusual decoration or a striking pin, rather than an entire hat out of shimmering metallic thread. Although she did have her eye on a startling, metallic-gold sheath-dress she'd seen in Liberty the week before… With a dress like that, no one would even notice what was on her head. She had tried it on, and it had slipped over her slim form like…well, molten gold, to misquote the hat buyer. She wondered what her mother would think of it; she would probably denounce it as far too *outré* – this seemed to be her condemnation of most of the current fashions. Alice hadn't even been able to persuade her mother to give up her corset – though how she could bear to wear such a restrictive undergarment in summer, she couldn't imagine.

'Alice, dear, do concentrate,' came her mother's tired voice.

'Sorry,' said Alice, 'what did I miss?'

'We'd like you to try on one of the winter hats. It's a little early in the year, but I'm trying to get ahead of the seasons and not have a repeat of last year when demand so far outstripped our supply capacity.'

'Don't you think it's good to have a shortage?' asked Alice. 'It makes the hats seem more desirable.'

'Miss Alice may have a point,' said Billy Francis. 'I'm not sure *The Lady* would have featured that ostrich-feather hat if it had been too readily available.'

'Pricing is everything,' said Alice's mother. 'If we keep the pricing above the…*more affordable* options, we will ensure our product remains a coveted accessory.'

Alice knew that 'more affordable' was her mother's way of saying 'worn by the lower-middle classes'. Despite her own success with the Debonair Designs hat business, her mother had a deep-rooted suspicion of those who had come to their money through hard work alone.

The business itself had begun as a millinery service for gentlemen. Alice's father had inherited a tailoring business in Savile Row, and when a thriving hat company had come on the market, he had seen it as a logical expansion. However, it hadn't been long before Alice's mother – naturally creative – had begun to sketch designs for ladies' hats. She had persuaded him to produce a small number of her designs, to test the market. Liberty, Harrods and John Lewis department stores had all placed orders, and the ladies' hat division had sprung into full production.

'Alice, do get a move on, dear,' came her mother's voice again.

'Sorry, sorry!' said Alice, fiddling with a hat pin, which seemed determined not to puncture the thick felt. She abandoned the pin and hurried out from behind the screen.

'Well?' said her mother, poised with a pen and notebook at the table.

'It's very…brown, isn't it?' said Alice.

'Well, it is a brown hat!' said her mother, putting down her pen. She sounded exasperated.

'Yes, but…'

'Brown is set to be the big colour for the autumn season,' said the molten silver lady brightly.

'Exactly,' said Alice's mother. 'And don't forget, Alice, that you are not representative of our typical client. She is a rather more traditional lady. She is not looking to stand out, but merely to present an elegant and stylish, yet traditional, image to the world.'

'What about this bow?' asked Alice, holding up the trim.

'What about it?' asked her mother.

'It dangles.'

'Yes – that's the design, you see.'

'It blocks my vision.'

'Ah. Perhaps we can make it smaller and raise it slightly,' said her mother. She drew a quick sketch and scribbled some notes.

'It really is very kind of Miss Alice to help out today with the modelling,' said Billy Francis. He was a creep, Alice decided.

'Yes,' said her mother, 'it was most unfortunate that Lily let us down like that.' She turned to Alice. 'Thank you, darling. Run along now and meet up with your friend – please apologise to her on my behalf, for detaining you.'

Alice ran back behind the screen to remove the brown hat, and quickly adjusted her hair before the mirror. Her new bob was a little tousled, but she felt she could carry it off. She re-applied her red lipstick and slipped out of the room. As she passed the board table, the creep and the buyer were debating the qualities of brown over maroon. She felt like asserting that both of those colours were offensive and should be worn only by the colour-blind or the almost-dead, but she restrained herself.

She checked her watch as she ran to the lift: there might just be time to persuade Suzanne to accompany her to Liberty before closing time.

Chapter Two

Hattie the Labrador took her head off Fleur's lap and began to growl quietly.

'What is it, girl?' With regret, Fleur tore herself away from the letters – and her dreams of a glamorous romance – and back to the present.

The dog ran to the back door and began to bark. Fleur got up to see what she was so excited about. Through the window in the door, she saw a red post van driving up to the house.

'It's ok, girl: it's only the mail.'

Hattie raced through to the hall, her paws skidding on the wooden floor as she turned out of the kitchen and scrabbled with her claws for a foothold.

'Slow down!' Fleur laughed.

The doorbell rang and Fleur went to answer it. She had to hold Hattie back by the collar, to prevent her from leaping up at the post woman.

'Just the one today,' said the woman, holding out a large, rectangular envelope.

'Do you need a signature?'

'No. I just wanted to deliver it in person – it looks like beautiful-quality paper. Look at the gold edging and the watermark on the envelope. I've been delivering these all morning around the village, and no one will tell me what's in them. It must be something very important.'

'Right… Well, thanks,' said Fleur, waiting for the post woman to place the envelope into her outstretched hand. She did so reluctantly.

'Must have cost a bomb. I wonder what the event is,' she said.

'I have no idea,' said Fleur pleasantly. 'I haven't opened it yet.' She stood and waited in silence, until the post woman gave up and returned to her van, swinging it around the turning circle with almost reckless casualness, one hand on the wheel and the other dangling from her open window.

Fleur carried the envelope back through to the kitchen and put it down on the table. She didn't really feel like opening it – it was probably just some publicity stunt by one of the businesses in the village, most likely the estate agent, hoping to tempt locals into selling their homes, and buying more expensive ones. As a buyer had already been acquired for her mother's house, there would be no need to attend.

As the youngest of four, the others of whom were settled in relationships, Fleur was generally indulged by the rest. Their mother's passing seemed to have hit her the hardest, and they were all keen to support her. In fact, she had received so many invitations to stay with them, she had started to wonder if she ought to look for a new home at all, or just live with them each in turn – perhaps spending four months with each one.

She looked around the kitchen, with its covetable Aga. The room smelled of her mother: a mix of laundry softener with nutmeg and ginger. It was a familiar, comforting scent.

'Time for a walk,' she announced.

At the word, *walk*, Hattie ran to get her lead, which she brought back and dropped at Fleur's feet.

'Good girl.' She clipped the lead to the dog's collar and led her to the back door, where she slipped on her own walking shoes and they set off down the driveway.

At the end of the drive, she stopped for a moment, ignoring Hattie's insistent tugs on the lead. The windmill next door had a 'sold' sign outside.

The windmill had been up for sale for months now, and although plenty of viewers had been by, none had been interested in purchasing.

She'd overheard one couple discussing it after a viewing: 'It's not just the fact all the rooms have curved walls, but all those stairs!' said the woman, with a laugh.

'I know! Good luck to him, finding a buyer for that one,' replied her companion. 'I only agreed to see it because the agent was so insistent. It began to sound like he was going to hold back on showing us other houses until we'd looked at the windmill.'

'Seriously? I wondered why you'd booked us in to see that place. Honestly – what a nightmare.'

The couple had moved out of sight, and Fleur had been left to wonder at people who failed to see the beauty in a place like Ferndene Mill. She was the first to admit that the mill was impractical: indeed, she couldn't argue that the curved rooms and steep wooden staircase would suit any but the brave or foolhardy. But the views... How could that couple have failed to mention the glorious scenes, visible from every one of those windows?

And now it was sold. Somebody had recognised the beauty of the place. She wondered who her new neighbour might be.

'All right, girl,' she said, giving Hattie her head so that she found herself almost yanked down the lane towards the river.

After a few moments of being dragged along by Hattie in an undignified fashion, she brought the dog to a stop, and removed the lead, so they could each go at their own pace. Hattie raced ahead along the well-loved path to the river bank. A loud, distant splash told Fleur that her dog was going to be wet and no doubt covered in smelly river weed and mud by the time they headed home.

Fleur took her time, loving how blue the sky was above the white froth of cow parsley along the lane. It was a glorious day – one that couldn't fail to lift even the most forlorn of spirits. She was humming a song to herself and performing a few steps from a country dance she'd learnt in school when her reverie was interrupted by a loud, angry cry from the direction of the river. The man's voice continued and she picked up her pace and ran towards the river. Whoever this was, he was furious with someone. She only hoped...

Too late. A contrite Hattie stood, head down, before the bristling form of a tall man whom Fleur didn't recognise.

As she ran towards them, the man rounded on her.

'Is *this* yours?' he demanded, pointing to Hattie, who slunk over to the safety of Fleur's side. There was no point in pretending otherwise:

'Yes, she's mine. Why, what's she done?' Even as she asked, Fleur took in the state of the man. He was covered in large, chocolate-colour paw prints.

'Oh no, did she do that?' she asked, pointing to the prints on his expensive-looking cream sweater and trousers.

'She did,' he said grimly. 'You really ought to keep an eye on her, and not let her jump up at people like that.'

'I'm so sorry – it's just that the only people here are normally other dog-walkers, so they don't wear their good clothes…'

'It stinks,' he informed her. 'What the hell is this stuff, anyway?'

'River mud.' She considered claiming that it was very good for the skin and that he should smear it all over his face, but she doubted he'd go for that.

'I'm so sorry!' she told him. 'She just loves to greet people.'

'Well, you should train her out of that. Not everyone *loves* to be greeted.' He checked his watch. 'Oh, great – now I have to get changed before leaving for London.' With that, he swept off, striding towards the lane without a backward glance.

Fleur looked down at the formerly sandy dog, now covered in chocolate mud.

'Go on, girl,' she said wearily, 'you might as well have another dip.'

Hattie gave a grateful yap as she ploughed back through the mud and into the river.

What a grumpy man, thought Fleur, as she dug her hands into her pockets and stood watching her dog chase after ducks with the joy of a toddler. A tear trickled down Fleur's cheek and she brushed it away angrily: she wasn't going to let a rude man like that ruin her enjoyment of this beautiful afternoon. She wondered, idly, who he was – she knew all the villagers – and why on earth he was going for walks in his best clothes, and not in scruffy jeans and walking boots or wellies, like a normal person.

When the ducks seemed to have had enough of laughing at Hattie's failed attempts to catch them, she called her back, clipped on the lead and headed for home.

'A bath for you, when we get back,' she told Hattie, who looked quite dismayed at the prospect. 'And a long, hot bath for me tonight. I think I've earned it.' And maybe, she thought, she would allow herself to read the next letter, as a special treat.

Fleur curled up in her favourite armchair after the two baths that night. Hattie lay flat-out on the rug, making strange little dog-noises as she chased ducks in her dreams. Fleur hoped she was more successful when it came to catching imaginary ones.

The latest letter was still in its envelope. Fleur withdrew it slowly, savouring the slightly musty, leathery smell it gave off, from its many years in the leather folder. She unfolded it and saw it was a response from her grandfather, Henry, to Alice's previous letter. She took a deep breath and immersed herself in her grandparents' story.

Chapter Three

El-Gaish Road

Alexandria

Egypt

15 May, 1928

My darling Alice,

I am counting down the weeks until you will be on your way to joining me.

With regard to the crossing itself, a midwife on-board recommended that I try ginger, of all things, for the sickness, and she was quite right. Chewing on ginger root may not be a pleasant experience, but it was certainly a saving one. Whilst others retreated to their cabins, I found myself strolling the deck, enjoying the bracing sea spray. Pack plenty of ginger, and I am sure that you, too, will fare well on the voyage. If you cannot lay a hand on any, the crew on the ship will have some stored away, I am sure, as they are privy to the root's medicinal qualities in treating sea-sickness.

Here in Alexandria, I have had such a welcome – all open arms and dinner invitations.

You are quite wrong, however, to suggest that I have no time to miss you: I can't wait to introduce you to all my new friends, whom I trust will soon become yours as well. I shall be so proud to show you off as my bride!

You ask about hats. I am no expert in such matters, but a hat with a veil seems a little extreme. Certainly, I sport no such object myself. Should it turn out that we need such items in the hottest or dampest months, then I am sure we can procure them here.

As for Mrs. Florence's musical evenings, now that I am so far away, I actually wish I might attend one! Perhaps Miss Bell has learnt to sing in tune since my departure? I hope so, for your sake. Do you remember how I had to avoid catching your eye the last time we heard her sing, for fear of laughing out loud?

Please don't think your own life too provincial for me: I want to hear all about it so that I might imagine you in each setting, and feel that you are closer to me.

You ask about my work. The office is housed in a brand-new building. Picture a rectangular edifice, hewn from a white stone, which sparkles like marble in the Egyptian sunshine. There are windows all around and, in the cool interior, huge fans that whirr overhead. The workers themselves are dressed in traditional local robes of plain black or -white. There is a sense of everything being very fresh and clean. Having walked past some less salubrious enterprises, I can only say that I am proud to be associated with such a place. My own office is at the back of the building, with large windows giving on to a cool courtyard containing a magnificent fig tree.

I think I have found my 'right-hand man', as you call him. His name is Frederickson – Adam Frederickson – though he is known as 'Freddie'. He is a tiny man, with a great moustache, quite comical in appearance but very knowledgeable about the market here in Alexandria. What's more, he speaks Arabic, which is a real boon. He has lived here for some twelve years and is something of an expert on Egyptian culture. It is Freddie who did most of the hiring for the offices and store rooms, and the workers show him real respect because he is a fair manager, who really cares about their welfare. You will like him, Alice, I am sure of it.

As for the flowers at our wedding: I leave it entirely to you to choose. Pink, white, or even violent purple – I care only that I will be married to you.

Well, my darling, I must dress for dinner with my new area director, Mr. Rees-Little. His wife is Egyptian and very beautiful, by all accounts, so I am keen to see her and make my own judgment. I am quite sure her light will bear no comparison to my Alice's.

Au revoir, my darling – may time and the tides speed you back to my side,

Your loving fiancé,

Henry

***

1927

Henry had been in his job for only twelve weeks, but he was a quick learner, and his boss Johnny Faraday seemed pleased with him. Henry was convinced there was potential to expand the company's range of cars, and he found a ready listener in Faraday.

'Talk me through these new models you feel we should be producing,' his boss said one day when they were sitting at their desks in their smoky shared office.

'I've made some notes if you're interested?'

'Excellent – let's have them.'

Henry bent down to draw the folder from his briefcase. He took it over to Johnny, who gestured for him to take a seat opposite him. Henry felt suddenly shy and vulnerable as his boss opened the folder and spread out the contents on his desk.

Johnny gestured to a sketch. 'So this would be the women's model?'

'Oh – those are only rough,' said Henry, blushing.

Johnny looked up at him. 'Relax: I'm not expecting you to have a fine-art degree on top of your sales and business skills.'

Henry laughed. 'Well, that's a relief, anyhow.' He peered at the drawing. 'Yes – that's "The Curve" – a high-end convertible for the modern young woman.'

'So this is the men's?' Johnny held up a sketch of a lean, sporty car.

'That's right. I'm thinking of this as the dashing vehicle for today's young-man-about-town.'

'And what are you calling this one?'

'"The Dash".'

'Makes sense. Look… Would you mind if I held on to these for now? I'd like to show them to the directors at the meeting this afternoon.'

Henry cringed at the thought of his childish sketches being viewed by the big bosses. 'You couldn't just talk them through it? As you can see, I've included a breakdown of the estimated costs for production and distribution.'

Faraday shook his head. 'No: they need something visual to go on. I long ago learned not to put any business proposal to them, without some pretty pictures to accompany it.'

'So, you're going to put my idea to the board?'

Johnny ground out his cigar in one of his overflowing ashtrays. 'That's the plan. I'll name you as the brains behind it, by the way – I'm not running off with your idea and claiming all the credit myself.'

'Thanks, Johnny – that's great.'

Johnny nodded. 'Now, get back to those numbers, would you? I need those projections by two o'clock.'

Henry stood up. 'I'll get them done now. I've nearly finished.'

He finished the required sales figures in good time and passed them to his boss, who headed upstairs for the board meeting. Henry waited for Faraday to return, but there was no sign of him. It was nearly six o'clock when he gave up and headed home. The rain splattered on his windscreen, and the short journey seemed like many miles, as he wondered if he'd made a mistake in allowing Faraday to submit his proposal. When he got to bed that night, he dreamed of cars spewing from the doors of the Harpenden factory, each one already possessing a driver. As the drivers drove away, however, he saw that, where the back of each car should have been, there was nothing – the cars were just facades, like the stage sets in music halls. He awoke with the conviction that his idea was nothing but a flimsy, arrogant daydream that would not stand up to inspection.

***

'They loved it,' said Johnny Faraday the next morning. His ever-present cigar often made his speech hard to understand.

'What?' said Henry, too taken aback to be polite.

Johnny removed the cigar. 'I said, they loved it.'

'Who?' said Henry, stupidly.

'The directors, you nincompoop, who do you think?'

'I'm sorry, Johnny, it's just…' Henry stood up and paced backwards and forwards a few steps in each direction before turning abruptly towards Johnny and saying, 'Really?'

'Really. And don't act so surprised – you knew it was a good proposal.'

'Well, I thought it was, and then I started to have doubts...'

'It's not watertight, of course – but the directors have given the nod to the design team to draw up some roughs, and the materials division are going to come up with accurate costings for the parts. They think there really might be a market out there for your glamorous young drivers.' Johnny smiled at Henry, who ran a hand through his hair and said,

'That's fantastic... It's amazing.'

'I'm glad you feel that way – I have a feeling the big bosses are going to want your input on this project. Now, I have work to catch up on.' Henry sat back down at his own desk. As he pulled out his new Otis King calculator, his boss said, 'Oh, and Henry...?'

'Yes?'

'Well done.'

***

Palmsworth Hall was an imposing building. Henry pulled up his green convertible in front of the Hall's grand façade, and a man from the house ran down the steps to open the car door. As Henry dismounted, his host came out to greet him.

'Henry, dear boy! What a pleasure!' Colonel Winchmore placed his cigar in the corner of his mouth and shook Henry's hand heartily. 'So glad you could make it. Jemima will be delighted to meet you. Now, where is she? Jemima!' The Colonel's voice was so commanding, a pair of wood pigeons took off in alarm from a nearby tree. 'Ah – here she is now. Come and meet Henry Pemberton, my dear.'

A wisp of a woman came out on to the doorstep; smiling, she walked toward Henry with her hand outstretched.

'Lovely to meet you, Mr. Pemberton,' she said. Henry decided he liked her at once.

'Mrs. Winchmore,' he said, shaking her hand gently, 'A pleasure to meet you.' She had a delicate air that made him afraid he might break her if he weren't careful.

'Right, come in, come in,' said the Colonel. 'It's a bit chilly for the time of year, isn't it? We've got a fire burning in the parlour.'

'It's so kind of you to invite me,' said Henry, looking around as they passed through a massive hallway, filled with beautiful rugs and portraits.

'Nonsense, dear boy, nonsense. Tell him it's nonsense, Jemima – delighted to have you.'

'When we heard you were Cynthia's nephew, we had to meet you,' said his wife, with less volume but equal sincerity.

Cynthia was Henry's aunt by marriage. She had died two years previously, and he still missed her – she had been like a second mother.

The house was every bit as lovely as Johnny Faraday had told him. Portraits lined the walls, and highly-polished suits of armour stood like sentry men beside doorways.

He stopped to admire a large black vase, intricately painted with a design of flowers picked out in red and gold.

'Japanese, isn't it, Jem?' said the Colonel.

'That's right. My great-uncle brought it back. It's been in the house longer than I have.'

'It's beautiful,' said Henry. 'Your house is lovely.'

They proceeded into the parlour, where parquet flooring was offset by thick-pile rugs in rich hues. Dark-wood panelling lined the walls and reflected the light of the glowing fire from a large hearth. A huge painting of a woodland scene hung over the fireplace; it seemed to shine from within, with the almost unearthly light of thousands of bluebells.

Jemima flicked a switch and wall-lights came on all around the room. The woodland painting was the largest picture in the parlour, but Henry now saw that there were smaller pictures in abundance. The mantelpiece bore a host of family photographs.

'May I ask about the paintings?' asked Henry, after they'd taken seats in the brocade armchairs nearest to the fire. 'Did you inherit all of them?'

'They're all Jemima's,' said the Colonel.

'You mean…?

'She painted them. Darned talented, isn't she?'

'Amazingly so,' said Henry. 'I particularly love the forest scene, over the fireplace.'

'Has good taste, hasn't he?' said the Colonel to his wife. He turned to Henry, 'That's my favourite.'

'It's the bluebells…,' said Henry, gazing at the picture. 'It's as if they shine from the inside.'

'That's exactly the effect I wanted to create!' said Jemima. She beamed at him. 'The light was perfect that day: they simply glowed.'

The Colonel poured drinks. Henry sipped cautiously at his whisky. He was keen to make a good impression and had already decided to keep his alcohol intake low.

'How did you know my aunt again?' asked Henry, after a pause.

'Cyprus,' said the Colonel. 'I was posted there for three years.'

'She was my closest friend over there,' said Mrs. Winchmore. 'I miss her dreadfully.'

'Me, too,' said Henry.

'So, how are they treating you over at Luton?' asked the Colonel. 'Are those talented blighters still there? What were their names, Jem?'

'Mr. Sharpe and Mr. Stephens, I believe.'

'Yes,' said Henry, 'They're still there. It's so exciting to be working in the same place as those astonishing men – I've followed their designs in the press for years, even before they moved to Harpenden.'

'Have you caught a glimpse yet of that "Queenie" car they're meant to be showing off at Olympia, at the Motor Exhibition?' asked the Colonel.

'I sat in her,' said Henry, trying to hide his pride. 'At my job interview, my boss, Mr. Faraday, took me over for a closer look. You know Johnny Faraday, I think?'

The Colonel whistled. 'You lucky man. What I'd give for an opportunity like that. Yes, Johnny and I go way back – we were at school together. 'Course, he left without a qualification to his name. Didn't hold him back, though, did it? Always did have a gift for business. I remember his little…enterprises, shall we call them? One time, he sold the nurse's own cat back to her – I wouldn't have believed it if I hadn't seen it myself. Think he's developed some integrity since those days.'

'I'd hope so, too,' said Mrs. Winchmore. 'Anyway, dear, I don't think you should be speaking to our young guest about his boss in quite those terms.'

'Quite right, my dear, quite right.' He turned to Henry. 'Don't know where I'd be without her, you know – she keeps me in check.' He smiled fondly at his wife, and Henry felt a moment's envy for their closeness.

Over dinner, in a surprisingly intimate little dining room, the Colonel talked about the house.

'It's been in Jemima's family since the Dark Ages.'

'Not quite,' said his wife, with a smile.

'Well, you know what I mean. Anyway, far too big for the two of us, now the kids have flown the coop.'

'So, what will you do?'

The Colonel shrugged. 'Rattle around until our son has us incarcerated and takes over the place himself.'

'Incarcerated?' asked Henry.

'Oh, you know: sent off to wither in some old people's hole or other: one of those awful places where they make you sing all day and insist you take part in tea dances.'

His wife leaned over to pat his hand. It was a gentle reprimand. 'You know that's not going to happen, Frank. Tom is far too good a son to do any such thing.'

'Wouldn't blame him if he did,' said the Colonel good-naturedly. 'He won't want us old fogies around forever.'

Jemima shook her head fondly. 'I'm sure Tom will take great care of us, should it come to it.'

'Anyway,' said the Colonel, abruptly turning to Henry. 'We were wondering if you could use the place at all.'

'How do you mean?'

'Johnny Faraday mentioned the big bosses are planning a ball to launch "Queenie", and we've got bags of room here.'

'Really? You'd let Harpenden Motors hold the ball here?'

'Well, it's not so much about Harpenden, as about wanting to do something to support your career, as a tribute to your lovely aunt. She was so proud of you.'

Henry was speechless for a moment. At last, he managed, 'I can't express how grateful I am to you, at this kind offer.

Of course, I will need to check with Johnny, to make sure the directors haven't already settled on a venue. But this would be a wonderful setting to launch a beautiful car like "Queenie".'

The Colonel nodded in approval. 'Well, we'll see what they say, then. More wine, Henry?'

***

Suzanne was in a bad mood by the time Alice met up with her.

'I'm so sorry to be so late,' said Alice. 'You did get my message, that I had to do some modelling for Mummy?'

'Oh, I got that, all right. I've just had a rotten day.'

'Oh no – what's happened? Come on, come with me to Liberty, and you can tell me on the way.'

'Why Liberty?' Suzanne surveyed her shrewdly. 'Have you seen another dress you can't live without?'

'I might have done,' Alice grinned.

'All right, well just let me loosen my shoe strap – I have another blister.'

'Honestly, Suze – if you didn't insist on wearing a size smaller than your actual size…'

'…If you had clodhoppers like mine, you'd do the same.'

Suzanne was tall and slim, with skinny ankles and enormous feet that were the bane of her life. Alice watched her friend adjust the strap of her Mary Janes and place a folded handkerchief over the latest blister, to prevent more rubbing.

'Right, all done – but we'll have to get a taxi.'

'Suze, it's only down the road.'

'I am not arriving at Liberty with a pronounced limp and blood seeping from my shoe. You never know who might be watching.'

Suzanne was always on the lookout for her next boyfriend, in the hope of finding a lasting relationship. She considered good first impressions vital to her cause. Alice sighed. 'Right… I'll hail a cab.'

They arrived at Liberty in a flurry of rain that sent them scurrying from the taxi straight into the perfume department, where they navigated their way around assistants who seemed determined to squirt them with a variety of scents.

'Do you need to lean on me quite so hard?' Alice asked her friend, who had grabbed her arm and was putting so much weight on it, she was giving Alice pins and needles.

'It was your idea to come here. I was all ready to go for tea. Hold on – I like this one.' Suzanne smiled at an assistant, who obligingly squirted her proffered wrist with scent from a large glass bottle. Suzanne waved her arm around, then put her weight back on to Alice.

'Phew! You weigh a lot for such a beanpole,' complained Alice. 'Come on, let's take the lift up to dresses. I'll buy you tea afterwards in the café here if they're still serving.'

When they reached the dresses floor, Alice stopped in front of the glimmering sheath dress she'd been coveting.

'Is that it?' said Suzanne. 'Doesn't leave much to the imagination, does it?' The dress was sleeveless, with a scoop neckline. It was also rather short at the front – though it hung lower at the back.

'It's knee-length,' said Alice defensively. 'Well, at the back, anyway!' They both laughed.

'What will your mother say?' asked Suzanne dubiously. She imitated Alice's mother's voice: 'Alice, dear, I really don't think you should go out like that. It's unseemly – and you'll catch your death of cold.'

'Isn't it lovely, though? All shimmering gold.' said Alice, admiring the way the dress sparkled beneath the shop lights. She was conscious of beginning to sound like that awful hat-woman from her mother's work.

'Try it on,' said Suzanne. 'Look – there's an assistant.'

Inside the fitting room, Alice removed her modest grey wool, below-the-knee dress and drew the golden sheath over her head. It slipped over her like liquid, highlighting her figure in all the right places, and throwing light back up to her face. She drew back the curtain with a flourish.

Suzanne was sitting on a cushioned chair outside the cubicle. She gasped when she saw Alice.

'You have to get it,' she breathed, reverentially.

'I do, don't I?' said Alice simply.

They giggled like schoolgirls as they followed the shop assistant to the till.

'Mummy will be cross,' said Alice. 'She says she's going to cut my allowance if I keep buying "inessential items".'

'But it's an essential item,' objected Suzanne.

'It really is, isn't it? Now, I just need a party to wear it to.'

After Alice had paid, they took the lift to the top floor for tea, but the café was closed when they reached it.

'I'm gasping for a drink,' said Suzanne. 'Can we get tea somewhere else?'

They left Liberty, stepping out on to wet streets. The pavements were still busy, with people hurrying to get home for their dinner, or to meet friends after work.

'At least, it's stopped raining,' said Alice.

'My hat's still sodden from earlier,' complained her friend. 'I reckon I could wring it out and cause another downpour. I hope it recovers all right.'

'If not, let me have it and I'll have the workshop girls steam it back into shape for you.'

'I forgot you could do that.'

'I do have some uses.'

'Not many, though.'

'Cheeky madam!' They grinned at one another. The two young women had formed a strong bond in their days at boarding school, and very little could come between them.

Alice checked her watch. 'It's five-thirty. 'Isn't it a bit late for afternoon tea?'

'It's never too late for afternoon tea. I want a cream bun. How about that new hotel on Piccadilly?'

'Come on, then: still my treat.'

Chapter Four

Fleur was in the garden, snipping old roses from her mother's precious ramblers. There were still plenty of buds, and she looked forward to staying in the house long enough to enjoy the full flush of apricot and cream flowers before the new owners took over. She was sporting a mid-length floral tea gown which had been her grandmother's, together with her mother's 'gardening hat', which was wide-brimmed and also covered in flowers. She could hear her mother's voice:

'Just because something has to be practical, doesn't mean it can't be lovely.' This rule applied to all of her mother's belongings: from chintz tea cosies to bone-handled cutlery, everything was aesthetically pleasing. Fleur had admired her own reflection in the hall mirror before heading out to the garden. She looked more like a Victorian lady stepping out to gather blooms in her cutting garden, than a twenty-first-century woman about to deadhead roses.

Fleur heard a car approach along the gravel driveway. She straightened up.

'We're not expecting visitors today, are we?' she asked Hattie. The dog wagged her tail and raced off, barking, to welcome visitors or defend her property, accordingly.

Fleur followed the dog's barks over to where a beautiful old, silver Jaguar was pulling up outside the house. Fleur admired the car's sweeping lines. She knew, without seeing the interior, that it would have leather upholstery and a walnut dash. It was a thing of true beauty.

Her heart sank, however, when she made out the person inside: it was the man from the riverbank – the one whom Hattie had coated in mud. She hoped he wasn't here to claim dry-cleaning expenses.

He got out of the car and held out a hand.

'Hi, there. I'm Toby Sinclair.'

She removed a gardening glove and shook the proffered hand.

'We've already met,' she told him.

'Have we?' He seemed taken aback. Then he took in the excited figure of Hattie, bounding around the car and yapping excitedly. 'Oh… It's her.'

'Don't leave the door open, or Hattie will climb in. She loves cars.'

'Right…' He slammed the door hastily.

Fleur grabbed hold of Hattie's collar and held her back from giving any more enthusiastic welcomes to Toby. 'I am sorry about the other day, by the river,' she said, feeling she should get in her apology before the accusations started.

He shook his head. 'No, it was stupid of me to wear good clothes for a river walk. I just had half-an-hour to kill before leaving for the London train, so I thought I'd squeeze in a stroll.'

'She gets a little over-enthusiastic; especially around new people.'

'That's understandable.' He crouched down and spoke gently to Hattie, and she trotted over, standing perfectly still while he patted her. 'Pleased to meet you, Hattie.'

'How did you get her to do that?'

He seemed surprised. 'Oh, dogs seem to like me. My mum breeds retrievers. I just wasn't in the mood the other day – I'd had a bad piece of news the night before, and I needed a bit of peace and quiet.'

'I am sorry. About your bad news, I mean – and about Hattie's intrusion.'

'That's all right.' He smiled at her, and she found herself blushing. He had intense dark eyes – she hadn't noticed those before when he'd been berating her.

'Is that your car?' he asked, pointing towards the old stable, where the cream-coloured Chevrolet was garaged. Fleur had uncovered her that morning, feeling that the old car deserved to look out on to such a glorious day.

'Yes – she belonged to my grandparents.'

'It's a beauty.'

'Thank you. I love her. I'm hoping to take her out for a run while the weather's still warm.'

'Does it still run?'

'I hope so. No one's tested her for a while.'

'Let me know if you need any help. I know a bit about old cars.'

'Yours is wonderful,' said Fleur. 'I haven't seen one like her in ages.'

'Thanks. It's my dad's old car. I only take it out on occasion – I have a Land Rover as my work vehicle.'

Fleur noticed that the car, to Toby Sinclair, was an 'it'. To her, beautiful cars were all female. She supposed that came from her family's involvement in the car trade.

'Did you get my invitation?' he asked.

'Invitation?'

'Damn. I knew I should have hand-delivered them. It's just, I've been so busy with the move…'

'The move?' she echoed.

'I live next-door: Ferndene Mill.'

'Oh! I wondered who had taken it over! I love that place; it's really magical.'

'It is, isn't it?' They both looked over towards the white sails on the round tower. Wisteria and Virginia creeper clambered up the walls, and hollyhocks nodded in the slight breeze. 'The minute I saw it – even before I'd stepped inside – I felt like I had to have it; does that sound ridiculous?'

She shook her head. 'Not at all.'

'The views from inside are amazing…'

He caught her eye, and they gazed at each other for a moment in awkward silence. Then Toby said,

'You were supposed to receive an invitation in the post, inviting you to my house-warming party. I sent one out to every household in the village.'

Fleur remembered the unopened envelope she'd deposited on the kitchen table, having assumed it was an estate agent's gimmick. 'Oh! I might have it… Come into the house for a moment, if you have time.'

He checked his watch. 'I have about five minutes. There's a decorator coming to discuss paint colours at eleven, so I need to be back for him.'

He followed her into the kitchen, where she retrieved the envelope from the table.

'Is this it?' she asked.

'Yes, that's it.'

'I'm so sorry – I thought it was just some marketing promotion, so I didn't open it.' She took a mother-of-pearl letter opener and sliced the envelope open, drawing out an embossed card with a picture of a windmill at the top – more precisely, a picture of Ferndene Mill.

'It's tonight!' she said as she read the invitation.

'Can you make it?'

She thought about the evening she'd had in mind: a long bath, followed by weeping over a screening of *Sense and Sensibility* on BBC2. 'I think I might manage,' she said, with a smile.

'That's great. Anytime after seven is fine. I have to get back now.'

She walked him out to the driveway, where he gave Hattie a final pat before sliding back into his Jaguar and starting the engine; even at its ripe old age, it purred like the big cat for which the marque was named. Fleur let Hattie chase the car to the end of the driveway.

When the dog arrived back, panting and happy from the chase, Fleur patted her on the back and said,

'Are you going to help me pick out an outfit for a party?'

Hattie ran ahead of her up the stairs and waited panting to see which way her mistress would go. Fleur opened the door into her grandmother's bedroom, to investigate the contents of the trunk. As always, she was thrilled by the dresses she pulled out: BIBA minis and Chanel tweed dresses with matching jackets. She tried on three dresses, before fixing on a tailor-made, fifties' dress with a neat, fitted bodice and a full skirt, in a shimmering, midnight-blue tulle underlaid with blue satin. The skirt had layers of net underneath, to give it body. She even found matching satin shoes with a small heel. Her grandmother used to have her shoes dyed to match her dresses. The shoes were slightly tight, but hopefully, her feet would survive the evening. The finishing touch was a pair of her grandmother's malachite earrings. She checked her reflection in the full-length mirror in her grandmother's bedroom. The dress came to just below the knee, which kept it from being too formal for a house-warming party. The truth was, though, that Fleur loved to dress up, and she would have worn the outfit to go to the supermarket, should the mood take her. She felt, as her mother and grandmother had also felt, that a touch of glamour could never go amiss.

'I've been talking to you far more than is healthy,' she told Hattie, as she stood in front of the bathroom mirror, smoothing her hair into a chignon. 'Right, Hattie,' she said, as she finished, 'I've left the back door open, so you can run around the garden if you like. Just leave the poor rabbits alone. I'm only going next door, and I should be back in a couple of hours, all right?'

As she headed downstairs and towards the front door, she heard the dog's paws behind her, and the soft knock of metal on wood. Turning, she saw that Hattie had fetched her lead, and was trailing it hopefully behind her.

'Not now, girl, I'm sorry.' Hattie gave a sharp yap. 'No, girl, your name wasn't on the invitation.'

As she shut the door, she heard Hattie begin to whine. It was almost enough to break her already shaky resolution. She was about to plunge herself into a gathering of people, many of whom she might not know since she'd left the village so long ago.

'Right: let's do this,' she told herself, patting down her skirt on the doorstep.

'Is talking to myself better or worse than talking to the dog?' she wondered as she headed for the little wooden gate that connected her mother's garden with that of the mill. The scent of the honeysuckle was especially strong this evening, and she inhaled the sweet smell that was always, irrevocably, linked to Wisteria Cottage.

Chapter Five

22 Beaumont Street

London

28 May, 1928

My dear Henry,

First of all, I must give you a brief account of Mrs. Florence's latest musical soirée. I did laugh when you mentioned her niece, Miss Bell. It is quite bad enough that the young lady has no taste or ability whatsoever – but then Mrs. Florence has to inflict her lack of talent on all of her friends and relations! Miss Bell's aunt must be either deaf or have no taste herself – otherwise, she would not allow her niece to torture us in this way. Even Mummy looked as though she would have liked to laugh when Miss Bell attempted a run of high notes in her 'closing number'.

Now, I feel quite ashamed for being so cruel. She is really a very pretty young lady, and we all enjoyed the pleasure of watching her, I am sure.

We were then invited to be delighted with the young Miss Van den Bergh's harp playing. Her tutor Mr. Bernard accompanied her on the piano, and the two of them made eyes at each other throughout. I trust her parents will now have the good sense to fix her up with a new tutor –

preferably an old, ugly one, rather than this handsome young man.

I will not bore you by describing the rest of the recitals, which seemed to go on and on while I gradually slumped in my chair. Now and then, my mother elbowed me, and I sat up more correctly – but otherwise, I allowed my mind to wander. In particular, it enjoyed returning to the moment I first saw you: such a tall, handsome man, walking in with Mr. and Mrs. Shepherd. How curious I was, to discover the identity of this mysterious stranger!

Of course, the ball you threw a few weeks later, at Colonel and Mrs. Winchmore's, was every lady's chance to make an impression on that distinguished gentleman. You would be astonished, dear Henry if you suspected half of the preparation that went into our outfits and hairstyles in preparation for that evening. It still amazes me that you picked me out, from among so many glamorous young women, all eager to dance with you and win your heart.

I must put down my pen for today because Mummy wants me to accompany her on some errands, but I will write again tomorrow. Please write soon, my darling, and tell me all about your life there. Was Mrs. Rees-Little as beautiful as her reputation had promised?

Yours, always,

Alice

***

1927

'Who is that?' Henry nodded across the ballroom, to where a slender young woman with sleek dark hair glowed like the sun, in a dress that appeared to be made from liquid gold. The dress caught the light from the chandeliers and reflected it back in all directions. It seemed to Henry that every man in the room must be mesmerised.

Mrs. Winchmore adjusted her lorgnette and peered over the throng. The noise was already overwhelming, and she wished she could go to bed.

'I think that must be the Debonair girl.'

'I'm sorry?'

'The daughter of the people who run the millinery business, Debonair Designs. They sell to some of the big stores – Liberty, Selfridges, even Harrods, I believe.'

'I see.'

'Should I introduce you?'

At that moment, Henry spotted one of Harpenden's investors arriving. 'Thank you. Maybe later, Mrs. Winchmore – business beckons.' He walked over to greet a tall, stocky man with a protruding belly, who stood with his wife. She was a tiny little woman with an alarming lipstick-red smile, and yellow hair piled on top of her head. Her dress was décolleté in a fashion that Henry was certain was no longer in fashion. Having worked for some years in his father's fine-cloth business, Henry had made a practice of keeping a close eye on the fashions through the monthly purchase of *Harper's Bazaar* magazine – a habit which he was having trouble relinquishing, despite there being little call for an intimate knowledge of hats, hem lengths or necklines at Harpenden Motor Company.

'Mr. Saunders, so glad you could come. And your wife…'

'…This is not my wife,' said the man, abruptly. The woman's smile didn't falter. 'This is Lizzie,' he said, offering no explanation for her presence.

'My pleasure,' said Henry, taking her hand briefly. 'Let me get you a drink. Champagne?' He beckoned to a waiter, who was circulating with glasses of the sparkling wine.

'Oooh, champagne!' said Saunders' companion, reaching for a glass.

'Don't drink too much, Lizzie – you know how it makes you behave,' snapped Saunders.

Henry wanted to walk away. He was conscious of how much difference Dominic Saunders' backing made to Harpenden's plans to expand its range of models. But the whole situation – Saunders turning up with this brassy woman instead of his wife, and then insulting her publicly – he wished he didn't have to be polite to the man.

'So, Henry, talk to me about your job,' said Saunders, trimming a cigar acquired from one of the passing trays, and lighting it. He puffed out smoke and watched it billow over the heads of the other guests.

'Are you just going to talk business?' asked Lizzie. 'I thought we were going to have a good time.'

'Later, later,' said Saunders, distractedly, waving his cigar as if swatting her away.

'We're still waiting for a couple of other investors,' said Henry. 'Meanwhile, I know Mr. Faraday is keen to see you again.' He beckoned to one of the waiting staff. 'Could you please find Mr. Faraday and ask him to meet Henry Pemberton near the entrance to the ballroom?'

'Certainly, Sir.' The waiter handed his tray to another servant and strode off to carry out the request.

Johnny Faraday, Henry's boss, appeared very promptly. He looked dapper this evening, with his normally unruly hair smoothed back, and his suit neat and unrumpled on his large frame. On his arm, there was a slender woman with dark hair fastened in a knot at the nape of her neck.

'Henry, I want you to meet Vera, my wife.'

'I've heard a lot about you, Mr. Pemberton,' she said, with a smile, as they shook hands. Henry introduced Dominic Saunders and Lizzie. Mrs. Faraday possessed all the grace and tact that her husband, with his forthright, blunt manner, tended to lack. Whilst her husband monopolised Saunders by launching immediately into a loud explanation of the plans to extend Harpenden's range of vehicles, Vera engaged Lizzie in quiet conversation. Henry joined in the men's conversation, but he observed Mrs. Faraday from time to time. She didn't have a beautiful face, but her manner was full of grace, intellect and lively spirit.

'So, Henry, when are we going to go through everything?' asked Faraday, suddenly. 'Are the directors ready?'

'I've laid out the papers in the drawing room. We just have to wait for two other parties to arrive.'

'So, I'm guessing not all your guests tonight are Harpenden investors?' said Saunders.

Henry shook his head. 'Not at all. Many are suppliers for Harpenden or friends and associates of the company's directors. Some are guests of Colonel and Mrs. Winchmore, whose house this is.'

'Beautiful place,' commented Saunders. 'Shame about the outlook. What is it, North/Northwest?'

Vera Faraday overheard. 'I suppose it depends on which outlook you mean,' she said, pleasantly. 'With a house like this, the views are spectacular in every direction, so the outlook from the front becomes less important.'

'My wife, ever the diplomat,' said Faraday fondly, slipping an arm around her waist and kissing her cheek.

'Get off, Johnny, not here!' she said, but she was laughing.

Looking at Faraday with his wife, Henry remembered the golden vision he'd seen earlier, on the other side of the ballroom. He glanced around and saw the same young woman, standing quite close by, chatting and laughing with a group of other young people.

'Would you excuse me?' he asked. 'I must just catch someone. I'll come back to find you for our meeting in a few minutes, Mr. Saunders, if that's all right?'

As he moved to walk off, Faraday grabbed his elbow.

'Don't leave me with him,' he muttered.

'Sorry – I just wanted to talk to someone...'

'Well, it will have to wait.'

Henry stole a final look at the woman in gold. She caught his eye and smiled questioningly. Then he gave in to the inevitable. He put away his concern that she might leave the ball before his business obligations were over: after all, the ball was designed to launch the new model, 'Queenie', and announce plans for expanding the company's range. Anything more potentially pleasurable would have to wait.

As a result, Henry stood dutifully, talking politely to a growing group of businessmen, until all the investors had assembled and he was able to escort them through to the study, the use of which the Colonel had offered for the meeting.

This room had a more serious ambience than the ballroom. As well as a desk close to one wall, there was a long, teak table, which filled the middle of the room. A set of upholstered chairs lined each side of the table. The effect was that of a boardroom – which was perfect to fit the tone of this meeting.

While the men sat in the smart chairs and drank fine brandy, one of the company directors introduced the plans to expand Harpenden's brand by introducing two newer models for the younger market.

'And we have this young man here to thank for the idea,' he said, singling out Henry. 'He's already proven himself to be an asset to the team in Luton. We're delighted to have him on board.'

He finished his speech: 'To sum up, we at Harpenden Motor Company plan to strengthen the company's brand, with the addition of these new models. With your backing, gentlemen, we can build an even more profitable enterprise, whilst still retaining Harpenden Motor Company's luxury edge.'

Johnny Faraday took over, detailing the company's plans in terms of export sales.

After the presentation was finished, they all stood up to leave the room. However, Henry found that his duties were far from over. Several of the men detained him in the hallway, asking further questions, only some of which he was equipped to answer. He referred two of the men to Johnny and attempted to answer the others.

At last, most of the investors seemed satisfied, and they all walked back towards to the ballroom. Henry found himself alone in the hallway with Saunders, who appeared in no hurry to get back. He finished his cigar slowly while studying the portraits that hung along the walls.

'Do you reckon these are all the ancestors?' he asked as he peered at a tall painting of a woman in a long, velvet dress, with a little dog at her feet.

'I imagine so…'

'Right,' said Saunders, with a loud sigh. 'I'd better see where that Lizzie has got to. Just hope she isn't plastered.' He laughed loudly though Henry failed to see the joke.

'I'll show you back to the ballroom,' he said.

They continued along the hallway, Saunders stopping regularly to estimate the value of a particular painting or ceramic artefact. Henry, who was stunned by the beauty of Palmsworth Hall and its contents, didn't know how to respond.

As they approached the ballroom, two elegant manservants swung open the doors and Henry was able to take in the scene from above. The six huge chandeliers sparkled and sent prism-rainbows around the walls. Beneath them, women spun in dresses the colour of precious stones: rubies, emeralds and sapphires.

One woman shone brighter even than the others, in a dress like molten gold.

Henry swiftly escorted Saunders over to Lizzie, who was desperate to dance. Then he shook Saunders' hand and bowed a farewell to the other businessmen, before rushing over to find Mrs. Winchmore. She was sitting, chatting with a group of elderly women who all wore long, fussy pastel dresses.

'Oh, there you are, Henry. How is it going, my dear?' she asked kindly.

'The meeting went wonderfully thank you, Mrs. W.' He gave her a hug and she squeezed his hand. 'This is our lovely, newly-adopted nephew,' she told her friends. She turned to Henry. 'You don't want to hang around with us old fogies. If the boring part of the evening is over, aren't you going to dance?'

'You did say you might introduce me…'

'Oh, of course! Just help me up, dear.' She made her excuses to her friends and took Henry's arm so that he could escort her over to 'the Debonair girl'.

'If only I could remember her name…' she murmured. 'Sally? No… Sarah…? I know Alice!'

At the sound of her name close by, the young lady in question turned towards her.

'Mrs. Winchmore! You have such a beautiful house! And what a wonderful evening.'

'Thank you, my dear. I'm glad you're enjoying yourself. Now, here's someone who's keen to meet you – the man who is responsible for throwing this ball. This is Henry Pemberton. Henry, this is Miss Alice Debonair.'

'Oh – that's just the company name,' said Alice. 'My family name is De Bonneville.'

Henry shook hands with her. She wore long, black gloves, which reached nearly to her elbows.

'Would you care to dance?' he asked her.

'I'd love to.'

He escorted her to the dance floor, where he discovered that her dancing was as charming as her appearance: she glided over the floor, responding to his slightest pressure as if she could read his mind.

At one point, she leaned in close, 'People are watching us,' she said, in an undertone.

'Is that bad?'

She smiled and arched a perfect eyebrow. 'Only if we get a step wrong.'

'We'd better not go wrong, then, had we?'

They danced to three tunes in a row, before Henry escorted Alice from the dance floor, and called to a waiter for some drinks.

The Colonel strode over to address him. 'Henry, dear boy, you have duties, you know,' he said. He whispered in Henry's ear, 'She is quite bewitching, but you mustn't neglect all your other guests.'

Henry felt torn. He desperately wanted to remain with Alice, to hear her talk and laugh. Her laugh was an uninhibited peal, which he found delightful. The Colonel was right, however: he had duties, as one of the hosts, to ensure the guests were all comfortable and entertained.

'Don't worry – you can leave me, you know. I won't vanish at midnight,' Alice reassured him. 'And even if I did, you do know my name: you'd have more than a glass slipper by which to track me down.'

The reference to midnight reminded Henry that the grand presentation of the new 'Queenie' car was yet to take place. 'Will you come out to see the new car?' he asked.

'Of course. She is the belle of tonight's ball, isn't she?'

'She has a serious rival on that score,' he said and saw her blush delightfully. 'Can we meet again?' he asked impulsively. 'I'd love to take you out.'

'I'd like that very much,' she told him.

Henry took his leave of her with a lighter heart after this exchange – he had met an angel, and she had agreed to see him again.

Just before midnight, everybody filed outside, to where 'Queenie' stood, draped in silks. On the stroke of midnight, strings were pulled to unveil the car in all her glory. Bright lights focused on her gleaming curves, and the guests gasped and murmured appreciatively. Henry sought out Alice and stood beside her as fireworks went off, like hundreds of shooting stars.

The ball continued until well past midnight. Henry saw Mrs. Winchmore, asleep in a chair, despite the noise. The next time he passed her, the Colonel was covering her tenderly with a shawl, tucking it in around her, to keep out draughts. He caught Henry's eye.

'Fifty years we've been together,' he told him, in a whisper. 'And she never ceases to surprise me. She's a wonderful woman.' He looked down at her. 'Fancy her managing to sleep through this din!'

'I hope it's not been too much for you both?'

'Not at all, dear boy, not at all. It's been delightful to see the old place full of life again.'

'It's been a wonderful evening for me,' said Henry. 'It looks like we may now have investors on board for the new models.'

'That's wonderful: congratulations. Faraday knew you were the man for the job, the moment he met you.'

'Did he? That's good to know...'

'She's still here, by the way,' said the Colonel. 'That girl in gold. And you've done your duty by your other guests now, I think. I hear the White Garden is bewitching at this time of night.' With a smile on his face, he nodded towards the ballroom doorway, where a small group of young people was milling. Alice still glowed among them, in her gold dress.

'I'm not sure it would be appropriate for me to escort a young lady out into the dark...'

'Oh, well, there's always the terrace – nice breeze out there, and you'd still be visible from the ballroom. Perfectly respectable.'

Henry took the hint. He strode over to where Alice was standing, chatting with her friends.

'Hello, again,' he said.

'Hello.' She smiled up at him. He felt as if they were the only people in the room – everyone else faded away. Did she feel it, too? It was as though there were a magnet, fixing his gaze to hers. 'Would you like to step outside for some air?'

'Oh! I'm just leaving – I'm waiting for my parents. The servants are bringing our wraps.'

'Oh...'

'Sorry! I've had a lovely evening.'

'Saturday,' he said.

'Saturday?'

'Come dancing with me at The Ritz.'

'I'd like that,' she said simply.

Two servants arrived, carrying piles of coats and wraps, which were allocated to the various members of Alice's party. Alice's own wrap was in the same shade of gold as her dress. Henry escorted them all out. Alice and her parents got into a chauffeured Bentley. Even as the car drove off, he could see her, shining like the sun, reflecting the lights from the great house.

Chapter Six

'Hello there! Welcome! Where's Hattie?' Toby was standing outside the mill, a glass of wine in each hand. Fleur felt suddenly self-conscious as he watched her approach. The dress boosted her confidence, though – it felt as if a little bit of her grandmother's spirit was woven into the lovely cloth.

'Oh… I didn't think she'd be welcome. You know how bouncy she gets.'

'She can bounce to her heart's content out here: there's acres of space. Shall I fetch her?'

'That's kind, but imagine…if she knocked someone's drink out of their hand or muddied their dress…'

He frowned, thoughtfully. 'Perhaps you're right. I feel mean, though – it's not as if we got off to the best start, she and I.'

'Oh, she doesn't bear grudges – it's all water off a dog's back to her.'

He laughed. 'That's good, then. Perhaps we can take her and Dougie for a walk together at some point. He's around here somewhere – have you met him?'

'Dougie?'

'My wolfhound. He takes life very seriously. He could do with a bit more bounce.'

'You have a wolfhound?'

'That's why I wanted a property with plenty of outside space. It's like keeping a small horse.'

They stood for a moment, without speaking. Toby's gaze was as intense as before, and Fleur could feel a blush spreading along her collarbone.

'Well, I'll look forward to meeting Dougie,' she said, at last, to break the silence.

Toby seemed to recall that he was the host for the evening. He broke off eye contact and nodded towards the back of the mill, where a crowd of people had already gathered. 'Look, I'd better deliver these drinks. Come on over and meet the troops. Watch out for the muddy spot over there in your party shoes.'

He gestured to a patch of earth, and Fleur was careful to avoid it. She felt suddenly self-conscious, arriving on her own. If Toby hadn't spotted her, she wondered if she might have turned and headed straight back home. Instead, she followed him dutifully around to the back of the mill, where the garden sparkled with white fairy lights. Some were strung between the weeping willows which lined the stream, whilst others shone out from the shrubs and flowerbeds.

'Oh!' she exclaimed.

'Do you like it?'

'It's beautiful.'

'I'm glad – it took me hours to get them all strung up. And Dougie was no help at all – he just stood watching me, with an 'I could do it far better' expression on his long face.'

'Well, it was worth it – it looks gorgeous. It'll be amazing when it gets dark.'

He grinned at her. He walked over to a man and woman, who were standing in earnest conversation beside a small fountain, which was also lit up. The water sparkled in the light.

'Drinks, Sir, Madam,' he said, mock-bowing as he handed over the glasses.

'What took you so long?' asked the man. 'We've been dying of thirst here.'

'It's a hard life you lead, Bill. Can I introduce my neighbour, Fleur Cavendish? Fleur, this is Bill The Martyr and the lovely Elise.'

'What a beautiful dress,' said the woman to Fleur. 'Is it vintage?'

'I suppose it is,' said Fleur. 'I hadn't thought of it like that. It belonged to my grandmother. I have a whole trunk of her clothes in the house.'

'Fleur lives next-door,' said Toby. 'Bill works in the City, and Elise is an interior designer.'

'And what do you do, Fleur?' asked Bill.

'I'm an illustrator.'

'Are you?' said Toby, staring at her. 'I hadn't realised.'

'We hadn't really talked about what we did,' she said.

'No, I suppose we hadn't. Look, I'll get you a drink, and then would you like a tour of the inside?'

'I'd love one. I haven't been in this place for years.'

'You have been inside before, then?'

'When I was little. There was a lovely couple who used to live here, Mr. and Mrs. Fatheringham. They would have an Easter egg hunt in their garden every year for all the village children. And on Christmas Eve, they would open up the house for a big meal, and invite everyone. They would string fairy lights everywhere in the house, rather like you've done out here, except that the lights would be multi-coloured. There was always an enormous Christmas tree in the entrance hall. As a child, the whole thing felt magical. We wouldn't all fit around the dining table, so there'd be small tables set up all over the house. I loved it – I think everyone did.' She became aware that she was the only person in the group who was talking. 'Sorry – I didn't mean to prattle on.'

'Not at all,' said Elise. 'It's fascinating – it sounds like an idyllic childhood. I grew up in North London, which was nice enough, but nothing like visiting a mill on Christmas Eve with all of your neighbours.'

'It was an idyllic childhood, pretty much,' agreed Fleur. 'The school was tiny, and we spent a lot of time out of doors, learning the names of trees and wild flowers – that kind of thing.'

'I'm getting nervous,' said Toby suddenly.

'Nervous? Why?'

'Because I'm scared I might have done things to the mill that will wreck your wonderful memories. Would you rather just stay in the garden?'

She laughed. 'You don't seem to have taken a bulldozer to the place, so I think it's all right. I'd love to take a look around, but not if it's going to worry you.'

'I tell you what, why don't you go on alone?' he suggested. 'That way, you won't have me watching your every movement for signs of trauma.'

'If you're sure, then I will: thank you.'

'There are drinks on the table in front of the house – help yourself,' he said. 'I'm going to stay here, and chew my fingernails while I wait for you to come back.'

She wandered over to the front of the mill. This was just as she remembered: Virginia creeper still scrambled over the walls, and the door itself was the original dark-oak, arched at the top and with a black metal latch. She smiled at a couple of other guests as she helped herself to a glass of white wine from the drinks table, and took a sip.

'So far, so good,' she murmured to herself, lifting the door latch and stepping inside.

Chapter Seven

El-Gaish Road
Alexandria
Egypt
27 June, 1928

My darling Alice,

The wedding preparations all seem to be in order – I am in awe of how much your mother has managed to arrange, whilst remaining in England. It would appear that her authority carries as much weight here, as in her own domain. There are flowers on order; the finest hotel restaurant in Alexandria has been booked for our reception, and the cake is to be a feast for the eye as well as the palate. I am sure, however, that your mother has done nothing without your approval – I am simply writing to reassure you that proceedings are well in hand, and you need have no concern of delays at this end. All that is needed now is for the beautiful bride to arrive. I keep telling myself that you will be on your way to joining me in fewer than five weeks – but it's hard to remain patient.

The church in which we shall be married, Saint Mark's Church here in Alexandria, is quite intimate in size. It has a

*delightful domed ceiling and lovely columns in white marble. I
think (hope) you will like it.*

*I did laugh at your description of the concert at which Miss
Bell delighted only herself (and perhaps her aunt) with her
recital! I have to confess, that I am not sorry to have missed it
(except, of course, for the opportunity it would have afforded
me, to be with you).*

*As for Mrs Rees-Little, she is, indeed, a beauty – though
I was right to think she could not hold a candle to you.
However, Mr Rees-Little is clearly besotted, so perhaps we are
each a little biased as to the perfection of our own beloved…*

*I am due downstairs shortly, for dinner with my host
family, who have been very kind to me since my arrival. They
are Egyptian, but the husband speaks good English, and is
always happy to explain local customs to me. He works in
the GM offices, as a manager on the administrative side. As
such, we are able to travel to work together in the morning.
Johnny Faraday's lure of a 'free car' seems to have been in
his own imagination. However, I have hired a car for now.
I am hoping to buy one after your arrival: we can choose it
together. The firm has promised me a good price on one of our
own models.*

*You asked me in a previous letter about the house with a
veranda, that I have found for us. I wanted to make some
improvements to the general layout and structure before you
came, but I am afraid that the work progresses at a slow pace.
The supplies are seldom delivered to time, and the builders
seem a little too keen to take breaks. They arrive late, leave
early, and take a long break in the middle of the day when the
heat is at its most intense. This is, of course, understandable,
but it does add to the delay. I am still hoping it will all be
finished before you arrive – though I may have to bring in
some extra workmen to complete the job. Once the work is
done, it should be a very pretty house indeed.*

My neighbour's son, Asif, has just knocked, to say I should go down now for dinner. All that remains is for me to tell you that I am missing my Alice, much as I would miss a limb – your absence is a constant ache.

Yours,

Henry

***

1927

The band was playing a waltz. Alice was sitting at a table beside the dance floor, watching the leisurely, rhythmic movement of the dancing couples, and hoping the band would soon switch to playing something more lively. It was no coincidence that many of the couples dancing were over forty – younger people rarely danced to anything as banal as a waltz nowadays.

Henry had jumped up to greet someone he knew, and now he led a young couple towards her.

'Alice, I want you to meet Vera and Teddy. They're old friends of mine from college.'

'Less of the "old", if you don't mind,' said the man, with a grin. He was tall and lanky, with a thick moustache and sleek, black hair. His partner was a brisk-looking woman, wearing a fitted skirt-suit in a pale-green tweed – an unexpected choice for a ballroom.

'Hi, I'm Vera,' she told Alice. As they shook hands, Alice considered Vera's style. She wore her thick, dark hair in a neat chignon – yet, somehow, she managed to make the whole outfit appear chic, rather than staid.

Alice was wearing a knee-length, black fringed dress, which her mother had pronounced, 'A bit funereal.' Alice herself loved the way the fringe swung as she moved. She had dressed it up with jade earrings and a matching choker, which highlighted the green of her cat-like eyes. On her feet, she wore a beautiful pair of snakeskin shoes in the same shade as her jewellery.

She had invited her friend Suzanne over while she prepared herself for this date.

'Are you sure you want to go for black?' Suzanne had asked, scrutinising the fringe dress Alice was wearing.

'You're starting to sound like Mummy. You're not going to complain it looks like I'm going to a funeral, are you?'

Suzanne shook her head thoughtfully. 'No, I'm just thinking that this man first clapped eyes on you when you were wearing the gold shift. He'll be remembering you as this gilded creature – he might get a bit of a shock if you turn up all in black.'

'I'm going to add my jade.'

'Hmm. That might work. Let's see.'

'Here – help me with the clasp, would you?' Alice held out the necklace and lifted her hair, and Suzanne obligingly attached the choker. Alice added the matching earrings, and Suzanne stepped back, to get a better look. She gestured for Alice to do a twirl, and Alice obliged.

'Well, it's not as sparkly as the gold, but it's still quite dramatic,' Suzanne declared.

'Thanks, Suze – you're a pal.'

'So, your mother is letting you go out on your own, unchaperoned? My mother would rather have me fitted with a chastity belt than allow me out unaccompanied.'

'She did try to object, but Daddy is a bit more liberal, thank goodness. He knew Henry's father or uncle or someone, so he said it was all right.'

'You are lucky. So, tell me: has Mr Henry Pemberton any handsome friends?'

Alice adjusted the fall of her skirt in front of the full-length mirror. 'I thought you were going out with that boy from Maida Vale – what was his name, James Lanchester, wasn't it?'

'Oh, I am,' said Suzanne, perching on the end of Alice's bed. She pulled a face. 'He's just a bit…boyish, if you know what I mean? I think it might be time to try stepping out with a proper, grown-up man.'

'I do know what you mean – that Maida Vale set are all so silly, aren't they?' agreed Alice.

'Whereas your Mr Pemberton seems very grown-up and sensible.'

'Oh, I hope he's not too sensible,' said Alice, with a shudder. 'We won't have anything to talk about otherwise.'

'The day you have nothing to talk about, Alice De Bonneville, is the day a pig flies over a blue moon,' said Suzanne.

Alice laughed. 'That's probably true. But I do hate having to work too hard to keep a conversation going – it's so tiresome.'

She needn't have worried, though – she and Henry had barely experienced a moment's break in conversation since he'd come by her house at seven o'clock to collect her in his car.

Even her father had been impressed by the vehicle when he'd opened the door to inspect the young man calling for his daughter. 'Nice car,' he'd said, forgetting to check out Henry as he peered over his shoulder. 'Quite smart, those Austin Sevens, aren't they?'

'Thank you, Sir,' said Henry, holding out his hand. 'She suits my purposes, all right. Good to meet you, Sir. I'm Henry Pemberton, here to collect Alice.'

Alice's father continued to peer past Henry, at the Austin Seven convertible, so Henry said, 'Is Alice ready?'

'You are a lucky chap. I have to drive a staid old thing – family car, you know?'

Henry had nearly pointed out that he felt pretty lucky to be taking out Mr De Bonneville's lovely daughter – but he stopped himself in time.

'Alice! shouted her father. 'Young man on the doorstep with a very smart vehicle.'

'I hope the vehicle's not on the doorstep,' said Alice, stepping out from a side room and taking a wrap from the hall table. 'Hello, Mr Pemberton.'

'Hello, Miss De Bonneville. Are you ready to go?'

'All ready.' She picked up a tiny clutch bag that matched her shoes. Henry, with his experience in his father's cloth business, was observant with regard to such details. Alice was less flamboyant in her black dress and jade jewellery than she had been in the gold number, but he thought her even prettier than he'd remembered. There was a delicacy to her features that was exquisite. Her lashes were long and dark, framing her vivid green eyes which stood in contrast to her very dark hair. He realised he was staring, and looked away with a blush. Luckily, Alice's father appeared not to notice.

'Have her back by eleven, would you?'

'Of course, Sir.' Henry escorted her down the steps to the car, where he opened the door and she slid inside as gracefully as a ballerina.

'You look lovely,' he told her, as he started the car and drove smoothly away from the house.

'Thank you. Not too funereal, then?'

'Funereal? No, not at all.'

'I think Mummy was worried you'd think I was making a statement about your company or something – you know, that I was deliberately looking dull because I was expecting you to be dull.'

'I can't imagine your ever looking dull.'

'Why, thank you, Mr Pemberton. Now, before I forget: do you have any handsome friends?'

He laughed. 'Why? In case I turn out to be dull after all?'

'Sorry – I should have started by explaining that I have been charged by my dear friend Suzanne, to find out if you have any eligible male friends.'

'Is Suzanne the young woman who was wearing a red-and-black dress with a gold sash at the ball?'

'My, you do have a good memory, Mr Pemberton. Yes, that's the one.'

'It comes from being reared in the cloth trade: I have been trained to notice attire. My father would have had my guts for gaiters if I'd ever failed to notice what a young woman was wearing, and especially the cloth from which it was made. Your friend's dress was a silk chiffon, if I remember correctly?'

'Very good. So – any friends?'

'Hmm. I'll think about it. There are a couple of young men at work who seem nice enough: good families, pleasant company.'

'Handsome?'

'I'm not the best judge of that, but they don't seem to have any shortage of young women happy to go with them to the cinema.'

'I see. I think Suzanne was hoping for someone a bit more serious.'

'More serious?' He raised an eyebrow. 'I do know an undertaker.'

'Now *you're* not being serious!'

He grinned. 'Sorry. I shall give *serious* consideration to your friend Suzanne's requirements.'

'That's better. But you mustn't tell her I've said anything to you.'

'Secrets already? And the evening has barely started.'

Alice didn't respond; she was too busy grinning out of the window – there was something about this man that made her excited, happy and nervous all at once.

Now, she focused on the couple who had greeted Henry with such enthusiasm.

'Mind if we join you?' asked Teddy. 'Only all the other tables are a bit far from the dance floor.'

'Oh…' said Henry. He looked apologetically at Alice, who smiled reassuringly and gave a nod. 'Yes, of course,' he said, without enthusiasm.

Vera hesitated. 'I'm not sure…' she told Teddy.

'What? What is it, Vee? There's plenty of room at their table.'

Alice caught her eye and they both laughed at how slow Teddy was to catch on.

'You might as well join us now,' said Alice, and Vera gave up and sat down.

She leaned towards Alice. 'He really can be very dim… Is this your first time out with Henry?'

'It is, yes.'

'I am so sorry to crash in on you like this – must be a frightful bore for you.'

'Oh, don't worry. It's nice to meet some of Henry's friends. One doesn't normally get the opportunity.'

'He's a good man, is Henry,' said Vera, quietly. Then she cried: 'Oh, they're starting a Charleston – shall we get these men on their feet?' Despite Teddy's protests, Vera, laughing, dragged him over to the dance floor. Once his feet touched the sprung ballroom floor, he lost his louche, slightly gawky air, and became graceful. He and Vera were wonderful to watch, although Alice didn't get much chance to sit and admire their dancing, because she and Henry followed close behind.

He led her over, and they were soon laughing out loud at how much fun it was to just give in to the music and dance the funny steps. Henry was as good a dancer as Alice had remembered. They seemed to move as one being – and this time, when a waltz came on, she didn't mind. It felt good to be held close by this handsome, interesting man. He wasn't quite like the boys she'd dated until now – he seemed more mature, more ambitious, and more full of enthusiasm for life.

Now and then, Vera whirled past her with Teddy, and she and Alice waved to one another. The dance floor was large, but it was busy. When it became rather too crowded, Henry leaned into her ear,

'Would you like to take a break?'

'Definitely.'

They held hands as they walked back to the table – and it felt as if his large hand had been moulded to fit around the exact shape of her small, gloved one. She felt almost frightened by how right it seemed, just to be with Henry.

When they reached their table, Henry said,

'Let's have a drink, and then do you fancy getting some air? We could go for a walk.'

'That sounds nice.'

They were both laughing as they downed their drinks – recognising the same eagerness in the other one, to be alone together. Vera and Teddy arrived back at the table, just as Alice and Henry were getting up to leave.

'We're off,' said Henry. 'Thought we might go for a walk, head towards the River.'

'We'll come with you,' said Teddy. Vera grabbed his arm as he moved to follow Alice and Henry.

'No we won't,' she said. Teddy looked bemused, and Alice felt sorry for him.

'We'd like to go together, if that's all right – just the two of us, I mean,' she explained gently.

'Oh, right…' said Teddy. He smacked his forehead. 'Have I been missing signs all evening, as usual?'

Vera stood on tiptoe to kiss his cheek. 'You have, my darling Ted, but that's all right. We love you anyway.' She turned to Henry and Alice. 'Now go, with our blessing. Shoo!

'Shall we take the car to the River?' Henry asked Alice, as they walked through the foyer of the Ritz, past the reception desk, where smartly dressed young women handed out keys and nodded silent instructions to porters to take baggage to the rooms. The ceiling was high, with huge crystal chandeliers, and the cream carpet was like soft fleece beneath their feet.

'Why don't we leave the car and walk from here?' suggested Alice. 'We could walk through the park.'

'All right, then,' agreed Henry. The doorman opened the door for them and they stepped outside. The exterior came as a shock after the refined interior: the air was thick and grey, from the smog seeping into central London from the industrial areas. As they walked along Piccadilly towards Green Park, it was hard to see far ahead of them.

'It's like we're in our own special bubble of time,' said Alice.

'That's similar to what I was thinking,' said Henry. 'It's as if the smog parts just enough to make room for us and no one else. Hey, are you cold? You're shivering.' He took off his jacket and draped it over her wrap.

'Thank you,' said Alice. 'It seems ridiculous, to be shivering in August.'

'Well, this is England. The climate is nothing if not predictably unpredictable.'

Alice laughed. 'True…'

They found the gates to Green Park and stepped through. The first awkward silence of the night developed as they wandered through the cotton-grey world. It occurred to Alice that her mother might not approve of her walking alone in the dark with a near-stranger. She had felt so close to Henry earlier in the night, that it came as a shock to feel a gap opening between them now.

Then Henry spoke: 'Alice…'

'Yes?'

'I would love to see you again.' He placed a tentative arm around her shoulders and she moved closer to the warmth of his body. They stopped walking and he turned her to face him, tilting her chin as he bent down and kissed her – as gently as the brush of a feather – on her lips.

'I'd like that,' she said, breathlessly, waiting for him to kiss her again. But he straightened up and held out his arm for her to slip hers through.

'Now, it's nearly ten-thirty and I made a promise to your father,' he said, as she accepted the proffered arm. 'I don't think it would look too good if I didn't get you back on time, do you?'

'Probably not.'

They walked back towards the Park gates.

'You've gone very quiet,' said Henry. 'Are you all right?'

She couldn't say that she wanted, desperately, for him to kiss her again – that she had never before been kissed with so much tenderness. She couldn't tell this man – who was still in reality a near-stranger – that she felt like she belonged beside him, that she wanted to stay here, hidden in the fog with him, and that she didn't want to go home.

'I'm fine,' she said.

'Alice,' he said, 'You feel it, too, don't you?'

She felt her chest contract with the anxious hope that he meant what she wanted him to mean. 'Feel what, Henry?'

'That we were meant to meet, somehow. That we belong together…'

She couldn't find the words to answer him, so she squeezed his arm instead and he said, 'Thank God, Alice, my darling. Thank God.'

Chapter Eight

Fleur shut the mill door behind her and paused for a moment, taking in the scene before her. The front door led, as always straight into the kitchen, where the curved walls had been freshly whitewashed. The cosy room was decked out with an Aga stove, and paintings of pretty interior scenes hung on the walls. Brightly coloured cushions padded the seats of wooden kitchen chairs placed around a rectangular oak table. Out of the little, cross-hatched windows – which were framed by red-and-white check curtains – Fleur could see the views across the garden to the wheat fields beyond. It was a lovely spot.

A sound came from behind her – a low bark – and she jumped and turned, to find herself confronting a very grave wolfhound.

'Ah – you must be Dougie,' she said softly. He didn't seem threatened by her presence: he simply walked over and they examined one another. He was a beautiful dog: thick, grey fur covered a large, muscular frame, and he had lively intelligent eyes.

'You're like a polite host, greeting his guest,' she remarked. His tongue shot out, and she corrected herself: 'Except that polite hosts don't normally lick their guests' hands.' She laughed and patted his back. 'Hello, Dougie, you're rather lovely, aren't you? Are you going to show me around?'

He barked once, as if he understood, then walked to the foot of the staircase and waited for her. The staircase was just as she remembered: it followed the curve of the exterior wall in a long, smooth arc. The old stair carpet – which had been a little worn even in her childhood – had been removed, and the wooden boards beneath sanded and polished. She and Dougie walked up together, he a little ahead, leading the way. He didn't stop on the first floor, which had formerly been the top floor of the house, but continued up the staircase, which now extended its sweep up, to a mezzanine level. Fleur thought back, remembering how the first floor used to have a loft-style ladder, leading up to a storage area. Now, the new half-floor was lined with bookcases. She climbed up and admired the view from a large window, which even boasted a padded window seat.

'It's like something out of a Jane Austen novel,' she told Dougie, as she took a seat and sipped at her wine. Down below, she could see the heads of the guests at the party. There was still some daylight outside, but the sun was beginning to stripe the sky in glorious shades of pink and orange: it would soon be dark. The fairy lights in the garden would really come into their own in the dusk. Toby glanced up from among a group of guests and saw her; he waved, and she waved back. Several of the guests turned to see who he was waving to, and she waved to them, too.

'Now I really do feel like the lady of the house,' she told the dog. He sat beside her, and she stroked his wiry fur as she admired the interior. Above her head, the vaulted wooden ceiling had been revealed, in all its rustic beauty. Again, as in the kitchen, the walls were hung with lovely paintings. She stood up to look more closely at an oil painting of a woman in profile who, with her elegant dress and glossy dark hair, made Fleur think of her grandmother,

Alice. Other paintings depicted landscapes in vibrant oil paints, or delicate watercolours of gardens, which reminded her of Monet's 'Waterlilies' series.

The bookcases had obviously been built to fit the space: they were curved to nudge against the rounded walls, and were so tall, a ladder had been supplied, to allow access to the upper shelves.

She peered over the edge of the balcony-style rail. The ground floor seemed a long way down, and she was grateful for the rail. The whole place seemed both familiar, and changed for the better. Every alteration Toby had made, simply served to highlight the building's charm. She had to admit that the Fatheringhams, although excellent hosts, had neglected the old structure, allowing some sections to rot, and covering up some of the wonderful features – such as the vaulted ceiling.

She descended the staircase slowly, deciding not to invade Toby's privacy further by peeking into the bedrooms. Instead, she and Dougie returned to the ground floor and made a detour via the living room – which, with its long, curved window and pale duck-egg-blue paint, made the most of the light streaming in, and highlighted the marvellous views. Then she and the dog walked back through the kitchen to the front door, where she glanced around at her surroundings one more time, before heading back out to join the party. There were far more people milling about outside than when she'd entered the house.

'Well?' Toby appeared out of the twilight, a tall shadow in front of her, and she jumped. 'Oh, I'm sorry! I didn't mean to give you a scare.'

'No, I'm too jumpy by far. I found Dougie, by the way.' She looked at the huge dog, who was wandering off towards the fields. 'Or I think he found me.'

'Was he stuck in the house? Poor old Dougie. Did he give you the tour, at least?'

'He did, indeed. He's an excellent host. What a lovely dog.'

'Yes, he's a bit too lovely: he's useless as a guard dog.'

'Well, there's not much call for that around here, at least. Most of the villagers leave their front doors unlocked when they go out.'

'Really? It's even nicer here than I thought, in that case… So…' He paused. 'What did you think of the mill? Have I destroyed the old place and ruined your childhood memories?' He looked nervous.

'It's gorgeous,' she said. 'It's as if you've brought it back to life, somehow.' She faltered. 'Sorry, that sounds stupid…'

He shook his head. 'Not at all,' he said, eagerly. 'Buildings do have personalities, don't they? Your own house is a friendly, jovial sort of place, isn't it? It welcomes you in. The mill is…' He searched for the right word, '…eccentric. It needed space to show off its individual character.'

She smiled. 'That's it, exactly! And I love the bookcases. And the window seat.'

'That's my favourite area – I always wanted my own library.'

'Have you read all of those books?'

'Most of them… Some I like to pretend I've read, like the Joyce or the Proust.'

They both laughed. There was a moment's pause. Then she said,

'I'm keeping you from your other guests.'

'Yes, we should get back. Let me take that empty glass from you. Come on, I'll grab us a couple more glasses of wine.' He put her glass down on the table and picked up two full ones. They walked around to the back of the mill, where the fairy lights shone like fireflies in the shadows.

Toby introduced her to some more of his friends, all of whom were friendly and welcoming. She was slightly in awe of how many people he had managed to summon to this mill in what most would consider 'the back of beyond'.

As the night wore on, she took herself off to a bench, from where she watched the guests move from group to group and listened to their laughter and chatter. She didn't know anybody well enough to want to plunge back into the midst of the party, yet there was something pleasant in observing from a slight distance. The evening was balmy, despite a clear sky. Soon, she would head the short distance home to Hattie. For now, though, she would sit for a while, enjoying the sense of being freed from her day-to-day routine.

Toby appeared – he seemed to make a habit of looming out from the darkness. This time, however, she didn't jump.

'Aren't you cold, sitting there in your lovely dress?' he asked her.

'Only a tiny bit. I was thinking how nice it was, just to sit for once, without anybody expecting anything of me.'

'I can leave you alone, if you like?'

She shook her head. 'No, it's fine: please join me.'

He sat down beside her, and they watched the guests together for a few minutes in silence.

'You have nice friends,' she said at last.

'Thank you. Yes, I'm very lucky. I can't believe so many came. I didn't think they'd leave London for anything, let alone for a party in…'

'…the back of beyond,' she finished for him, seeing his hesitation at using this potentially offensive phrase. 'It's all right – I know that's what most people think.'

'How long have you lived here, Fleur?'

'It's years since I actually lived here. I'm just here while we sell my mum's house. I was renting in London myself, until a couple of months ago.'

'So, you're not staying?'

'No. Once the house is sold, I'll have to get back to where the jobs – and my friends – are.'

'Do you not have friends here?'

'Not really. Most of them moved away after we finished sixth form. Their parents are still around, but it's not the same.'

'No, of course.' He paused. Then he said, 'So, I'd better be quick if I want you to show me the sights.'

'I would have thought you'd found most of them for yourself by now,' she said, with a smile.

'Well, I've found a very pretty cottage next-door, with a very friendly sandy Labrador and her owner. Does that count?'

'It's a start.' She grinned at him, and felt herself start to blush as they made eye contact. She thought, for a moment, that he might be about to kiss her. She wondered if she should let him – she hardly knew Toby, after all, and she had witnessed his rather bad temper by the river. What if he often blew his top like that? She felt pinned to her seat, suddenly aware of how near his face was, and how smooth his lips looked. She wondered what they would feel like against her own…

'Toby – that's where you are! We've been looking everywhere.' The woman who spoke had long, curly, russet hair. Earlier in the evening, she had been standing close to a string of fairy lights, and her face and hair had been lit by them, showing the exquisite cut of her features. She resembled one of the pre-Raphaelite paintings Fleur had admired at the Louvre gallery in Paris – all smooth, alabaster skin and classical profile.

'Sorry – I fancied a few minutes' peace and quiet.'

'Fine host you are!' The woman shook back her glossy curls and laughed. There was no reason to laugh, so Fleur could only assume she was trying to impress Toby. It would be interesting to see if he was so easily lured.

'Marissa, this is my next-door neighbour, Fleur. Fleur, this is my bossy friend, Marissa.'

'Hello, Fleur.' Marissa held out a limp hand, which Fleur shook briefly. 'What's it like, having Toby for a neighbour? Does he keep you awake with his banging?'

'His banging?'

'Oh, didn't you know? Toby's a stone carver – when he's not being an architect.'

'No, I didn't know that.'

'Mind if I join you?' Marissa didn't wait for an answer, but squeezed herself in between the two of them. As there wasn't really room, Fleur found herself pushed to the end of the bench. She stood up.

'Right – time I got back to Hattie. Thanks for a lovely evening, Toby, and for letting me see what you've done to the old mill – it's beautiful.'

He moved to stand up, but she held up a hand, 'No, don't get up – I only have to get through your side gate, after all. I think I can make it unchaperoned.'

Part-way across the garden, she glanced back. Marissa was sitting so close to Toby, she looked as if she might be about to climb on to his lap. Toby's body language showed that every inch of him was straining to move away without giving offence: he was leaning at a curious angle. Fleur felt a pang of guilt for having abandoned him with Marissa – then she remembered that he was the one who must have invited the intrusive woman to the party.

It was only at bedtime, lying in her quiet, cool room, with the curtains open to the stars, that Fleur remembered the almost-kiss and savoured the almost-sense of it on her own smooth lips.

Chapter Nine

                              22 Beaumont Street

                                   London

                              15 July, 1928

*My dear, dear Henry – too far away by miles – how I miss
you!*

*How I miss your ability to make me laugh when my mother
makes me want to scream. How I miss the way you smile
when I catch your eye in a crowded room. How I miss your
hand enclosing my own.*

*Time is dragging here. I feel as if I shall never board the ship
that will take me to you. If I have to go to one more recital,
courtesy of Mrs. Florence's too-kind hospitality, I swear I shall
scream. Do you know, last Friday, she actually invited her
mother-in-law to entertain us on the harp? This mother-in-
law (a tiny, rotund woman, in a too-small dress) has only
recently begun to learn! We had to sit through what seemed
an interminable number of wrong notes – nasty, squeaking
sounds – after which she took a bow, beaming as if she were a
protégée and had just performed at the Royal Albert Hall.*

*Enough of Mrs. Florence and her unskilled performers! The
house sounds truly delightful, my darling. It's hard to imagine
the two of us in our own home, with no intrusion from my*

well-meaning mater. She really is unstoppable at present, in her mission to ensure nothing is omitted that might help towards my future happiness and stability.

She keeps dragging me along to her Women's Institute meetings, where her friends regale me with stories of the horrors they have heard from their own acquaintances, who have returned from Egypt. Apparently, I should always cover my shoulders and knees – is this true, my darling? One lady even suggested that I should wear quite 'baggy' (her word) clothing, to avoid 'showing my figure'. The same lady stated that even ankles are considered shocking in some areas of Egypt! I can't decide whether these ladies are trying to scare me – or whether I have as much to learn as they suggest.

Of course, Mummy will accompany me to the wedding, so any rules that apply to me must also apply to her! I suppose, she does tend to dress rather more conservatively than I. However, I console myself with the idea that, had I chosen a more 'modest' dress to your ball at Palmsworth Hall, you might never have noticed me! What a horrendous thought, my darling – that I might have so blended into the crowds, that you and I would never have met! Perhaps you might have noticed Suzanne instead, and it would be she who would now be preparing to voyage the long distance to be by your side. No, I shudder to think of such a turn of events – I shall dash that image from my mind. Much as I love Suzanne, I must have you for myself.

I have stocked up already on ginger root, as per your suggestion. Mummy, Daddy and I will all have some to share, and I am hoping it will be enough to keep us well for the trip.

Tonight, we are to dine with my cousins in Kensington. I am sure you remember Louisa and Francesca, who are like sisters to me. They are such darlings, and always indulge me by allowing me to prattle on for hours about all your virtues. I shall wear the black dress with the fringes, which I wore the night you and I went to The Ritz.

I am so glad that everything is coming together for the wedding. Mummy is working so hard that I feel quite guilty, but she assures me that it is a joy to her, to plan her daughter's wedding. In my quieter, more reflective moments, I acknowledge that I truly am blessed, to be loved by so many wonderful people.

However, the majority of my own love, I confess that I reserve for you, my darling Henry.

With love,

Your Alice

***

1927

'I want you to come with me to the Motor Exhibition at Olympia this weekend.' Johnny Faraday stubbed out his cigar in the overflowing ashtray and glanced across the office to Henry, who was sitting at his desk, producing complex calculations for some large orders that had come in for the new models. According to Henry's sums, if all went to plan, they would need a lot of backing from investors. He balked slightly at the thought of being quite so indebted to Dominic Saunders – the man who had brazenly brought along a woman to the ball who wasn't his wife. However, they needed funds from external sources, and they couldn't afford to get too choosy about the social integrity of these sources.

Henry looked up from his calculations and nodded at Johnny, trying to look pleased with the thought of spending the weekend with his boss. His heart sank, however: he had been hoping to take out Alice that weekend, perhaps boating on the Serpentine, followed by a picnic in Hyde Park. He hadn't seen her since the previous week's outing to The Ritz, yet he couldn't get her out of his mind. She was like no woman he'd met before. So many young women nowadays were constantly sarcastic, in a misplaced attempt at wit and panache. Alice was vivacious and outspoken, yet rarely sardonic.

Henry knew how important it was to visit the annual International Motor Exhibition, to keep up-to-date on the latest trends in manufacturing and purchasing. However, he had been hoping to do this on Friday night. He would be a fool, though, to turn down the chance to go to the trade show in the company of Johnny Faraday – one of the industry's best-known figures.

'That sounds great,' he told his boss, mustering enthusiasm. 'Did you hear Francis Birtles is going to have his Bean Fourteen on display before he sets off for Australia?'

'Is that the chap who's planning to drive right across Australia? I wonder what modifications he's had to make to his car.'

'I've heard he's replaced the exhaust pipe and has had a large auxiliary fuel tank fitted.'

'Didn't he stencil kookaburras and such-like all over the paintwork? It's certainly going to be a distraction, among all those untouched new cars. Anyway, I want to have a close-up look at some of the new six-cylinders – that's where the main manufacturers are focusing at present.'

'I read that Erskine is going to present his new Studebaker, too,' said Henry.

'Oh, that,' said Faraday dismissively. 'He's fitted it with a Continental engine – cheaper than the Studebaker engine, but far inferior.'

' What about Chevrolet?' said Henry. 'They're lovely-looking cars. I can't find out whether General Motors are exhibiting a Chevy this year.'

'GM have been rather secretive about the 1928 Chevy Capitol AA they're about to launch… They're claiming it will give Ford a run for its money.'

'I hope we get a chance to see one.'

'Me, too. Right, let me have some figures by Friday, will you?' Faraday lit another cigar, and Henry resisted the urge to cough pointedly as the fug increased. Sometimes the air got so bad in there, it was as if a particularly bad smog had made its way into the office. Whenever staff knocked on the door, they would take a step back in shock as they opened it on to the ghostly landscape of smoke, peopled by the shadowy figures of Henry and Faraday.

***

'Alice, darling, when are you seeing that nice boy Jonathan again?'

'Mummy, Jonathan was months ago!'

'Really?' Her mother looked up in surprise from her newspaper.

'Can you pass the marmalade please, Mummy?'

Her mother handed her the little bowl across the breakfast table, and Alice spooned some of the orange preserve on to the side of her plate.

'So, who was the boy with the bicycle?'

'That was Danny Van den Berg.'

'A bicycle! I ask you! What use was that, to take a young lady out for the evening?'

'He was saving up for a car. He just wheeled the bike along, and we walked.'

'Very odd… He might have borrowed his parents' car. And then there was…' she squinted with the effort of remembering, '…the young man with the ginger hair…'

93

'That was Sebs.'

'Oh, yes! Sebastian Allen, wasn't it? Claude and Ginnie's boy?'

'That's right.'

'What happened to him? I liked him: he was very polite.'

'I'm not keen on his type.'

'His type?' queried her mother.

'You know puppies that stare at you with big, sad eyes, and follow you everywhere.'

'Don't be unkind, darling. He was devoted to you. Such a sweet boy.'

'If I wanted sweet, I'd put more sugar in my tea.'

'Sugar… That reminds me – I promised the WI I'd bake some cakes for the sale next Tuesday.' Her mother dabbed at her mouth with her napkin and pushed back her chair. 'All right, darling, I must get ready and go.'

'Where are you going?'

'Honestly, Alice, weren't you listening to anything I said? I have to pay a visit to old Mrs. Larkin in the corner house – her legs are playing up again. Then I must head to Steeple's and pick up some new stockings. Is there anything you need?'

'No, thanks.'

'You can come with me if you like. I'm sure Mrs. Larkin would like to see you – she still talks about that little embroidered pincushion you made for her when you were six. She has it in pride of place, on the sideboard.'

'All right, then. I'd like to see Mrs. Larkin – she's a darling.'

'Be quick, though: I don't want to be late. Let's meet in the hall in ten minutes, hats on and ready to leave.' Alice pushed back her own chair and stood up. Her mother looked her up and down, as if only just taking in what her daughter was wearing. 'Oh! Don't you think that's a bit short for daytime wear?'

'It's what everyone's wearing, Mummy. It's the latest fashion from Paris... or somewhere...' Alice was dressed in a knee-length shift dress in white lace, with a panel of crochet work in the centre of the bodice. Unlike her mother's own restrictive, corset-bound outfit – which came down to her calves – Alice's looser dress only skimmed her figure.

'I'm just not sure Mrs. Larkin will think it entirely... appropriate. She's quite an old lady now, and she isn't so tolerant of the new fashions...'

Alice sighed. 'Right... I'll change.'

'Would you, darling? I mean, it is a pretty dress...' her mother began doubtfully.

'...Just frightfully risqué,' finished Alice, with a laugh. 'It's all right, Mummy.' She walked over and kissed her mother on the cheek, before squeezing past her out of the breakfast room. 'I'll put on the blue floral you like.'

She headed up the staircase, and her mother called a 'Thank you' after her. Alice adored her mother, and would have dressed in one of the sacks the potatoes came in, had she requested it. As it was, there was no real hardship in donning the pretty blue dress covered in flowers, which came to a modest mid-calf length. Alice added a silver heart locket, and a light spray of a floral scent. She glanced at her reflection in the full-length mirror. Whilst not the height of fashion, her outfit was pleasing enough, and Mrs. Larkin would approve.

The old lady still lived in the house in which she had grown up – she and her husband had moved in there after her parents had died. It was a large, redbrick Georgian house, with Virginia creeper growing up the front. Alice loved the house, and its owner, whom her mother had known since her own childhood. The front door was opened by the maid, who showed them through the square hallway, filled with antique vases on highly-polished tables, to the large sitting room, where Mrs. Larkin stood up to greet them. She was dressed in an old-fashioned, high-neck blouse and long skirt, and, despite her tiny stature and advanced age, she still had a very upright, slightly prim air. Alice gave their hostess a hug, plus a kiss on her soft cheek, and then indulged the old lady's whim to treat her like a much younger girl. 'I have some sweets somewhere...' she said, rummaging in a drawer. 'I know what a sweet tooth you young ones have.' She drew out a round silver tin and took off the lid. Inside, were what looked like cough lozenges. Trying to hide her reluctance, Alice removed one of the dark-red bonbons and unwrapped it, thanking her hostess.

As Alice sucked nervously on the strong-flavour sweet, her mother and Mrs. Larkin struck up a conversation about the courting rituals of modern young people.

'Of course, the youngsters do it differently now,' said Mrs. Larkin, fondly. 'They don't even have to know the families beforehand. It's all changed since my day.'

'Yes, quite,' said her mother. 'To be perfectly honest, I'm not entirely sure which young man is Alice's suitor at present.'

As Mrs. Larkin looked suitably horrified, Alice said, through the boiled sweet in her mouth, 'It's Henry Pemberton.'

'Henry who, dear?' her mother asked.

'Henry Pemberton. You know, the young man who called to take me dancing last week.'

'Don't speak with your mouth full, Alice. Was there a Henry? Oh – was he the one with the car your father liked so much?' Alice nodded. 'I'm not sure that I met him,' continued her mother. 'He's not related to Virginia Pemberton, is he, the lady who died?'

Alice hesitated: she wasn't allowed to speak with the foul sweet in her mouth, yet she was being asked a direct question – one which it would be rude to ignore. In the end, she removed a handkerchief from her pocket and delicately removed the boiled sweet, under the guise of dabbing at her nose.

'Sorry,' she said and bestowed a charming smile on them. 'I believe that she was his aunt, Mummy.'

'Oh!' said Mrs. Larkin, 'A delightful lady! I was very fond of her – so sorry when she passed.'

Free now to drink her tea, which had been placed by the maid on a table at her side, Alice picked up the china cup and saucer and sipped at the still-hot liquid.

'So, this Henry,' said her mother, turning back to her. 'When are you seeing him again?'

Alice set down her cup and saucer. 'I'm not sure. He said something about this weekend.'

'I would like to meet him. Please make sure we are introduced when he calls for you.'

'All right, Mummy.'

The older women resumed their conversation, and Alice was free to daydream. She remembered how Henry had removed his coat in the park, and how warm it had felt around her shoulders – almost like an embrace. Then she remembered the real embrace, his lips on hers, and she shivered involuntarily with pleasure.

'Are you cold, Alice, dear?' asked Mrs. Larkin.

'No, not at all. It's lovely and warm in here.' In fact, the room was boiling – Mrs. Larkin had a roaring fire going, despite the heat outside.

'Oh, Alice, I have something I thought you might like,' said their hostess. 'I need you to fetch the box that's on my dressing table. You remember where my bedroom is?'

Alice nodded: she had spent many happy hours there, as a child, trying on the beautiful dresses and jewellery that were housed in Mrs. Larkin's wardrobes and cabinets. She got up and walked through to the bedroom. The room was just as she remembered it though the fine flock wallpaper had faded from purple to a pale grey. The purple curtains, too, had faded, though they still had their pelmets and tasselled tie-backs. There was the strong smell of moth balls, taking Alice right back to the days of her childhood, when Mrs. Larkin had drawn satin and silk dresses, scarves and gloves from her wardrobe, to indulge her little guest.

There were two paintings on the wall. These were familiar, and Alice stood for a moment to take in her old friends: a woman sitting in a field, beneath a large parasol; and an elderly woman, knitting before a fire. Despite the hot sun outside – and the fire in the living room – the bedroom was cold. As a child, Alice had stood before these pictures, sensing the heat of the fire in one painting, and imagining she could smell the grass in the field in the other.

She realised her mother and Mrs. Larkin would start to miss her, so she picked up the large, rectangular box that lay on the dressing table, and hastened back along the long corridor to the living room.

'Did you find it?' asked her hostess. 'Oh yes, there it is. Set it down on the central table, would you, dear?'

Alice did as she was told, placing the box on the round, glass-topped table at the centre of the room. She looked to Mrs. Larkin for further instruction.

'Well, open it, then!' The old woman smiled encouragingly.

Alice lifted the lid and parted the tissue paper inside. She gave a gasp as an ornate, white lace dress was revealed.

'Take it out.'

Gingerly, she lifted the heavy white bodice from the box; the white chiffon skirt fell in folds below it. The bodice itself sparkled subtly, with hundreds of tiny beads.

'It's beautiful!' she said, awed by the craftsmanship of the piece.

'It's Venetian lace, handmade by nuns' said Mrs. Larkin. 'It's my wedding dress. I thought you might like it when your time comes. We can have it altered, of course. There's a veil in a separate box.'

'Doesn't your granddaughter want it?'

'Violet chose a very simple, rather plain dress for her wedding,' said the old lady. 'But I had a feeling you might prefer something with a bit more pizzazz.'

'It's wonderful,' said Alice. 'I'm not engaged to anyone, though...' She thought of Henry and felt her cheeks flush.

Mrs. Larkin was watching her intently. 'No, but I have a feeling it won't be long,' she said, with a shrewd smile. 'A pretty girl like you...'

'I would love to wear this when the time comes...' Alice held up the gown and watched it catch the light. It was surprisingly heavy and beautifully made.

'It's yours,' said Mrs Larkin, simply. 'Just tell me when you need it.'

Alice caught her mother's eye. She also seemed to be watching Alice carefully.

'This Henry,' she said, 'You have only been out with him the once...?'

'That's right. Though we did dance at the ball at Palmsworth Hall.'

'Was that him? I see…' Her mother looked thoughtful, and Alice blushed again, realising she had made the connection between Alice's slightly distracted air, and the new young man in her life.

'Anyway,' said Alice, 'I'm sorry – you two were talking about the Women's Institute, I think…'

As the older women chatted, Alice's mind drifted back to a certain walk through Green Park, with a certain young man… By the time they took their leave and set off to Steeple's haberdashery store, Alice's head was full of thoughts of Henry Pemberton, and the hope that he would take her out again that weekend.

Steeple's was a well-stocked shop near Bond Street, selling a wide range of haberdashery and accessories. It had started as one small room, but its success had led to the gradual acquisition of neighbouring buildings. Inside, the store was now laid out as a series of rooms, each with its own products. Floor-to-ceiling drawers were labelled and alphabetised, like the shelves at a library. At the stocking counter, Alice's mother sifted through various silk stockings which the shop assistant placed on the counter.

'What do you think, Alice?' she asked her daughter.

'I think those would be a bit thick at this time of year,' said Alice, pushing one pair to the side. 'And these have a strange, shiny surface.'

'You're right – they do have a sheen: well spotted. What does that leave?'

Alice picked up a pair that had no sheen and were in a fine, lightweight silk. 'These would be my choice.'

'Excellent,' said her mother. ''ll take seven of this style, please.'

'Very well, Madam: a good choice – these should wear well. Will that be all?'

'Yes, that will be all for today, thank you.' She turned to Alice. 'I'm glad I brought you with me.'

'No hats, Madam?' asked the young woman at the counter. 'We have some very fine ones just come in, direct from Paris.'

Alice's mother caught her eye with a smile. 'Oh, those might be interesting – thank you.'

'If you would follow me, Madam.'

The assistant led the two women through an archway into the millinery section of the shop, where she handed over their care to a middle-aged man in a pinstripe suit.

'Madam; Miss,' he bowed to them. 'Melissa tells me you are interested in seeing some of the latest styles from Paris.'

'Yes, please,' said Mrs. De Bonneville.

'We have cloches, toques, fascinators…'

'Cloches,' said Alice at once.

'Very well, Miss.'

As he placed a variety of cloches on the counter, Alice picked up a teal-blue one with a turn-up brim and a self-colour ribbon. It was in a gauze-like fabric.

'This is lovely,' she said, removing her own blue felt cloche and drawing on the dainty teal one. 'What do you think?' she asked her mother, examining her reflection in one of the mirrors on the counter.

'It is lovely,' said her mother. 'Take it off – I want to see how it's made.'

Alice removed it, and her mother pored over it. 'Seam-free,' she said. 'I wonder how they stiffen the gauze…'

After a while, the two women became aware that the shop assistant was scrutinising them.

'I'm sorry,' said Mrs. De Bonneville. 'We aren't really here to buy hats, but merely to check out our competitors. I am the owner of Debonair Designs.'

'Debonair!' The assistant turned to two female members of staff, who were filling display shelves. 'Maggie and Mrs. Fillibrown, please come over here.'

The two women walked over, and the male assistant said, 'This lady is Mrs. De Bonneville, of Debonair Designs.'

'Oh!' said the young woman, whom Alice guessed to be Maggie. 'I love your designs. I have one of your hats.' She looked down, adding, 'I could only afford the one...'

'We have a sale coming up,' said Alice. 'You should visit our Bond Street store the week after next.'

Mrs. De Bonneville was looking at the young woman. 'Would you try this on?' she asked her, holding out the gauze cloche.

Maggie looked to the male assistant for permission, and he nodded. Then she pulled on the pretty gauze hat.

Mrs. De Bonneville nodded. 'If you would agree to do some modelling for us, then I will let you choose a hat from the new range.'

'Really?' Maggie's eyes grew wide.

Mrs. De Bonneville rummaged in her little handbag and drew out a card. 'My details are on here. Please drop in when you are available, and we can sort something out.'

She turned to leave, but as she did so, Alice said wistfully, 'I did like that gauze hat.' Maggie had removed the cloche and was replacing it on a display stand, with a pair of dainty teal gloves beside it and a matching bag.

'I am not paying for hats,' protested her mother. 'What would it look like?'

She caught Alice's eye and sighed. 'Very well.' She turned back to the counter. 'And we'll take the gauze cloche.'

Alice threw her arms around her mother. 'Thank you, Mummy! You are a darling.'

'You certainly know how to get around me,' said her mother, but she was smiling. She patted Alice's arm and took out her purse.

As they left the shop, Mrs. De Bonneville said thoughtfully, 'I think I might take a look at that hat when we get back. I'm interested in how they've managed to produce it to appear so delicate, and yet to be robust enough to keep its shape.'

'You're always working,' said Alice.

'I need to,' said her mother. 'How else would I keep you in hats?'

Chapter Ten

'Do you want to start with hats or shoes?' Tilly was standing in front of the gigantic trunk into which their grandmother Alice's clothes had been transferred when the wardrobes had been removed in the great family clear-out of a few weeks earlier.

'Shoes,' said Fleur. She walked over to peer into the trunk. 'I'm not sure they're in here, though – they must be in the box room. Shall we go and look?'

The two sisters walked across the landing and into the tiny room, with its sloped ceiling. This space had been crammed full of boxes, trunks and suitcases but, like the rest of the house, it had largely been cleared. There were, however, several stacks of shoe boxes along one wall.

'It's freezing in here,' said Tilly. 'Let's take the boxes back to the bedroom. You'd never know it was July.'

'This house always did have its own climate,' agreed Fleur. 'Do you remember that time it rained inside?'

Tilly, her arms full of boxes, shivered as she walked towards the door. 'There was only one slate missing from the roof, but you'd have thought it was the monsoon season,' she agreed, over her shoulder. 'In fact, didn't Grandma Alice say it reminded her of the rainy season in Egypt?'

'And Dad was joking about having to get the canoes out,' said Fleur, with a laugh, as she bent to pick up the remaining boxes and follow her sister out of the room.

Back in their grandmother's bedroom, they put down the shoe boxes and removed the lids.

'Snakeskin,' said Tilly, holding up a pair of shoes with a pointed toe and a high heel.

Fleur squealed. 'Those are the ones!'

'The ones what?'

'The ones I always wanted to fit me. But they never did.'

'Try them now.'

Fleur slipped off her ballerina pumps and slid her feet into the olive-green snakeskin shoes. 'They fit!' She danced around, and her sister laughed.

'Since when did you get so excited about shoes?'

'Since the pair I've always wanted finally fit on my feet.'

'Fair enough. Now, Cinderella, what shall I try?'

'How about these?' Fleur held up a pair of knee-length boots in a dark-brown suede; they had a block heel and were fastened by a series of buttons which ran the length of the boots.

'Those are lovely.' Tilly swiftly removed her strappy sandals and slid her feet into the leather. 'Oooh – they feel cold, though!' She tried to fasten the buttons. 'They're really stiff to do up.'

'Here,' said Fleur, holding up a slim hook she'd found in the box with the boots. 'This should help. I had one of these button hooks for my character shoes in ballet class.' She showed Tilly how to hook each button and draw it through its loop. When Tilly had mastered the technique, she fastened the remaining buttons herself and stood up.

'Now, all I need is a 1960s dress to go with them,' she said, admiring the boots in the full-length mirror.

'I think there might be a Mary Quant dress in here somewhere…' Fleur bent over the trunk and began to sift through its contents. 'It's hard to bend down in these shoes, though.'

'Yes, fashion and practicality rarely go hand-in-hand, do they?'

There came a thud and a cry from downstairs, followed by a wail, of 'Mummeeee'.

'I almost forgot the kids were here,' said Tilly, looking shame-faced. 'I've been having far too much fun.'

'Naughty Mummy!' said Fleur, with a grin. 'Are you going to tend to your wounded one?'

'Yes. Hopefully, I'll be back shortly.'

In Tilly's absence, Fleur unearthed a zip-front mini-dress in a brown suede, which boasted the label 'Jean Muir'. There was also a mini-dress in a design of large squares of black alternating with red; this one bore the 'Mary Quant' label. Fleur placed them on the bed, for Tilly's return.

As she rummaged, she uncovered a large, rectangular box. By the time Tilly returned, three-year-old Benjamin in her arms, tears still glistening on his cheeks, Fleur was decked out in a heavy, intricately beaded lace wedding dress, complete with veil.

'Who's the lucky man?' asked Tilly.

'Anyone who'll have me.' They both laughed.

Tilly set Benjamin down, and he ran over to the boxes of shoes. He pulled out a pair of sky-blue sandals with a high heel, and said,

'Me try?'

'All right, my darling,' said Tilly. 'Be careful in those heels, though, won't you?'

The women laughed as Benjamin teetered around the bedroom. It wasn't long before two more little faces appeared around the door, and Benjamin's sisters – Amelie, who was seven, and Genevieve, six – came to join the fun. Hattie the Labrador – who always appointed herself as the girls' bodyguard when they visited – followed behind. She quickly found a spot in one corner, where the warm summer sun streamed in and made a pool of warmth. She lay down and closed her eyes, content that the girls were now safely back with their mother and aunt, and her own work was done.

It took Fleur right back to her own childhood, as the two little girls exclaimed over the pretty frocks, and Genevieve – who was very stubborn – insisted on putting on three dresses at once, one over the other.

'You'll trip up, darling,' objected Tilly.

'She's just like her mother,' said Fleur, fondly.

'Is she?'

'Don't you remember? Grandma Alice had a terrible time persuading you to wear just one of those long dresses at a time. You had some theory that you could layer them up, and then hitch up the skirts to reveal the ones underneath – like pretty petticoats.'

'I'd completely forgotten! It was because of the pictures in my pop-up *Cinderella* book. Cinderella had a dress for the ball that was hitched up around the bottom of the skirt, showing a different fabric beneath it. I loved that dress!'

'I really envied you that book. Didn't it open out to form a whole scene, with the pumpkin coach and all the coachmen?'

'We've got that book,' said Amelie. 'Mummy only lets us look at it when she's there.'

'That's because it's so fragile,' said Genevieve.

'Fragile,' corrected Tilly. 'But what a good word to know.'

Fleur sat down on the floor to watch the dressing-up games, and Genevieve promptly plonked herself on her aunt's lap, her thumb in her mouth. The layers of long skirts trailed across the softly carpeted floor.

The doorbell sounded, and they all looked at each other.

'I go!' shouted Benjamin, staggering towards the door in the high heels.

'Benjie, no! You mustn't go downstairs in those shoes,' Tilly told him.

'I'll go,' said Fleur. 'I didn't do up the wedding dress. If Genny will get up, I've still got my normal clothes underneath.' Genevieve obligingly hopped off her lap, and Fleur peeled the heavy dress over her head and draped it back inside the trunk.

'Wait!' said Tilly, as Fleur headed for the bedroom door. Tilly strode towards Fleur and unclipped the veil.

'I forgot all about that!' said Fleur. 'Could have been embarrassing…'

Fleur ran downstairs, patting her hair into place. No one ever called on her – it was probably just the post woman.

'Coming, coming,' she called.

When she got to the door and wrenched it open, she saw Toby, heading back towards the connecting gate between her garden and next-door's.

'Toby, wait.'

He turned and strode towards her. 'I thought you must be out.'

'No, sorry – just trying on my grandmother's old clothes with my sister and her kids.'

'Sounds fun.'

There was a moment's silence, which she broke: 'Did you want something?'

'Some sugar?'

'Oh, right… Just come in for a second…'

As she rummaged in the kitchen cupboard for a bag of sugar, Toby explained:

'Sorry to intrude. It's just, I'm meant to be baking a cake for the village jumble sale. Only, when I opened my bag of sugar, it had gone all hard and caked together. It must have got damp at some point.'

'No problem: I've just got to find it! Ah: here it is.' She brought out a bag of granulated sugar and held it up to show him.

'Thanks.' He walked over and took the sugar. He made no move to leave, however.

'Was there something else?'

He sighed. 'I'm having a bad time with the farmer who owns the land at the back – do you know him?'

'Mr. Pargeter? Yes, a little.'

'Well, he says he has right of access to the mill pond, for his sheep.'

'Really? I don't remember the Fatheringhams – the previous owners – having to allow him access.'

'I've been right through the deeds, and I can't see anything about it.'

She thought for a moment. 'Look, my sister, Tilly went to law school – do you want to come up and ask her about it?'

He looked hopeful. 'Are you sure she won't mind?'

'She's a mother to three gorgeous children. She's generally delighted when somebody remembers she had a former life, as a person with a brain.'

He laughed. 'That would be great. Or I could wait here…'

She shook her head. 'No, you might as well come up. You could have a long wait before everyone's back in their normal clothes.'

She took him up and knocked on the door to her grandmother's room.

'Tilly are you and the kids decent?'

'All decent,' came the response.

'I'm bringing in a guest, in that case.'

Tilly had a look of mild alarm on her face as she took in the figure of Toby Sinclair, following Fleur into the room. She had donned the brown suede dress and added a hair band: if she'd applied some black eyeliner and false lashes, she could have blended perfectly into a documentary on the fashions of the sixties.

'Toby's our next-door neighbour,' explained Fleur. 'He's hoping you can drag your mind back to your pre-child-fogged days, to when you spoke legalese.'

'Thanks very much,' said Tilly, indignantly. 'It wasn't all that long ago. Only…seven…or eight years.' She closed the trunk and sat down on the lid. 'Oh my God: I've been out of the workplace for eight years.'

'I like the sixties get-up,' said Toby.

'I normally dress like a mum,' said Tilly.

'She always looks lovely,' said Fleur, loyally.

'Did you not want to dress up, too?' Toby asked her.

'Oh, I was doing. When you rang the doorbell, I was wearing that.' She pointed to the beautiful wedding dress and veil, which were lying at the top of the trunk.

'That's gorgeous. Is it Venetian lace?'

'I think it might be,' said Tilly. 'I seem to remember Mummy saying something about its being worked by Venetian nuns. How do you know about such things?'

'Oh…I have an interest in the origins of beautiful things.'

'Toby's an architect,' Fleur told Tilly. 'Do you remember me telling you about the wonderful job he's done over at the mill?'

'Thank you,' said Toby. 'That means a lot.'

'I'm so glad you've brought the old place back to life,' said Tilly. 'I always thought that the mill could be really lovely, in the right hands. What was it you wanted to ask me? I have to warn you, my legal knowledge is somewhat rusty, as you can imagine.'

'I'm having trouble with the farmer who owns the land behind us, and Fleur thought you might be able to advise me.'

'Go on…'

While Toby went through the details, Fleur went downstairs to put on the kettle. Her nieces and nephews followed her, and she found herself making ice-cream milkshakes to order.

'I want funny bits,' Benjamin told her, gravely. He had still not forgiven her for insisting he abandon his stiletto shoes at the top of the stairs. The girls, however, had been very good about leaving the dresses behind they seemed to have some understanding of how precious the clothes were.

'He means hundreds and thousands,' Amelie translated.

'Right. And how about you?'

'I don't like hundreds and thousands. Do you have any chocolate flakes?'

'I like flakes, too,' announced Genevieve.

Fleur found some chocolate flakes and crumbled them into Amelie and Genevieve's milkshakes. She shook hundreds and thousands over Benjamin's shake and placed them all on the old oak dining table, which was covered in a Liberty-print laminated tablecloth. *Just because something has to be practical, doesn't mean it can't be lovely*: her mother's words sounded in her head as she made tea in the large, spotty Susie Cooper teapot and poured milk into the matching jug, setting out the cups and saucers from the same set.

'Bikkits?' asked Benjamin. He had hundreds and thousands stuck to his cheeks, like some alarming rash.

'We might have biscuits in a moment or two if your mummy says it's all right.' She glanced at the girls. 'Amelie, please could you go up and ask your mummy and Toby if they'd like to come down for some tea?'

Benjamin slurped the dregs of his milkshake. 'Yummy-yummy.'

'I'm glad you liked it.'

'Yummy-yummy, choccy shake!' Benjamin shouted. He climbed down from his chair and began to run around the room, with his arms spread like an aeroplane. Toby appeared, and Fleur a few moments later, back in her 'mum clothes', which were nonetheless dainty and summery. As she entered the room, Benjamin careened into her.

'Sorry,' said Fleur. 'I fed him sugar.'

The adults watched the small boy race around the kitchen like a battery-powered toy on a full charge.

He stopped suddenly and turned to his mother.

'Bikkits?' he said, hopefully.

'I think you've had enough sugar, don't you?' said Tilly.

Without argument, he went back to running around the room.

'I've made tea for the grown-ups,' said Fleur. Benjamin started to climb on the sofa that stood in the pretty bay window. They all watched him for a moment.

'Is he ok doing that?' asked Toby.

'Oh, I learned long ago that I can't stop him from throwing himself into danger,' said Tilly, drawing out a chair and sitting at the table. 'I always carry antiseptic cream, plasters and bandages in my bag. The staff at A&E know him by name – and I've become an expert at applying a tourniquet.'

'My little brother was like that,' said Toby. 'He once threw himself through a plate-glass window.'

'Done!' said Fleur and Tilly in unison. When Fleur saw Toby's bemused look, she explained:

'Benjamin drove his ride-on tractor through those very French windows when he was two.' She pointed at the pair of glass doors that led out to the back garden. 'Mummy was minding him, and she felt awful. She had them mended afterwards, but with toughened safety glass.'

'So then he climbed out of a first-floor window,' said Tilly. 'Broken arm and seven stitches. We were lucky it wasn't worse.'

'Mum refused to mind him after that,' said Fleur. 'The girls could come on their own, but she said she couldn't handle the responsibility – or stress – of minding a trainee stuntman.'

'We've had to nail everything in our house to the wall or floor,' said Tilly. 'You'd be surprised what a determined toddler can use to have an accident.'

Fleur poured the tea into the spotty cups. 'Where are the girls?'

'They're upstairs, trying on the clothes,' said Tilly.

'Me try clothes, too,' said Benjamin, running towards the door.

Tilly leapt up and headed him off. 'No, not right now, darling. Auntie Fleur has some lovely paints over here. Let's see if you can paint me a rocket.'

Benjamin stopped. 'A halien.'

'Ok: an alien. What colour will he be?'

'Purple,' said Benjamin, without hesitation.

'Lovely. I shall look forward to seeing your purple alien.'

She settled him at the small table that Fleur had set up for painting. Then she came back to join Toby and Fleur.

'So, what happened about Farmer Pargeter?' Fleur asked.

'Your sister thinks I am probably in a strong position,' said Toby.

'If the deeds don't mention the farmer's right of access,' said Tilly, 'then I suspect it's just some verbal agreement, perhaps long in the past – possibly between the farmer's father, and whoever was then living at the mill.'

'But why has he suddenly decided he needs that access?' asked Fleur.

'A long, hot summer,' suggested Toby. 'His own pond may be dry. Mine is fed by a spring, of course, so it has a constant supply. I wouldn't mind giving him access if the sheep wouldn't make such a mess of the new shrubbery I've put in. In fact, I might suggest letting him run a pipe from the spring, to refill his own pool.'

'That's a good idea,' said Tilly. 'It's always better to settle disputes without involving legal experts, especially where neighbours are involved.'

'I'll talk to him tomorrow,' said Toby. 'Hey, why don't you all come to see my new planting scheme? It's early days, but I think it's going to be quite pretty. You could all come over later, for a picnic in the garden. The Lilac Path is lovely at the moment: it's having a second flowering.'

A shout from upstairs, accompanied by barking, alerted them to a crisis. 'Where's Benjamin?' asked Tilly, pushing back her chair and starting towards the door. A trail of purple paint led across the wooden floor, to the kitchen door and beyond.

'Excuse us,' said Fleur to Toby, pushing back her own chair and following her sister.

Upstairs, the two little girls were squeezed into a corner of the bedroom, screaming, as Benjamin advanced on them with palms that were wet with shiny purple paint. Hattie – who bore paint on her sandy-white coat – was barking excitedly, but seemed unsure how to resolve the situation.

'Benjamin, no!' shouted Tilly. Mindless of her own pretty floral skirt and pale-pink chiffon top, Tilly scooped up her son and strode from the room. Fleur surveyed the scene. Apart from the paint on Hattie's back, the damage seemed minimal. Then her eyes fell on the wedding dress, which she had left inside the trunk. The beautiful white lace bodice bore the vibrant purple print of a child's hand.

'Oh, no...'

'May I come in?' Toby was hesitating at the door to the bedroom.

'Of course,' said Fleur, gazing down at the damaged dress.

'What's happened?'

Fleur gingerly picked up the dress, holding it high for Toby to see the handprint.

'Oh, not the wedding dress,' he said.

Fleur felt tears prick at her eyes. She couldn't get any words out.

'Look, I'm going into town later,' said Toby. 'I can take the dress if you'll let me, and see if the dry cleaner can get the paint out.'

'It's quite old,' said Fleur, with tears in her eyes. 'I'm worried the fabric might disintegrate.'

'Don't worry – I know a really good place; they won't attempt to clean the dress if there's any danger to the cloth.'

Fleur nodded. 'Thank you,' she said gratefully.

Now that the coast was clear of the purple-paint monster, the girls emerged from their corner.

'Do you really think you can make it better?' asked Amelie.

'I can't,' said Toby. 'But I know a shop that does a very good job with beautiful old clothes, like this dress.' He took it from Fleur, and they all studied the intricate lace, still exquisite after so many years.

'Did it belong to your granny?' Genevieve asked Fleur.

'That's right: she was your mummy's granny, too. She was a very glamorous lady, with lots of lovely clothes. These were all hers.' She gestured to the box full of finery.

'I think we should put them all away now,' said Amelie, very seriously. 'We don't want any more of them to get dirty or torn.'

Fleur was touched by how carefully the girls removed the clothes they were wearing and replaced them in the trunk. The two children seemed much smaller without the layers of trailing gowns and high heels.

'Shall we go back down?' she suggested.

They traipsed downstairs, Toby leading the way with the wedding dress spread across his outstretched arms, purple stain upwards. The purple stain made the dress look more like a Halloween costume than a wedding dress. Fleur hoped the dry cleaner would be able to do something about the stain.

From upstairs, they could hear the bath running, and Benjamin's indignant protestations.

'I have to head off,' said Toby, as they gathered in the hallway. 'So I'll take the dress with me. But I shouldn't be long in town – how about that picnic in my garden afterwards? We could have an early evening meal out there, before the kids' bedtime.'

'It does sound nice,' said Fleur.

'Yayyyyyy! Picnic! Picnic! Picnic!' chanted the girls.

'Shall I take that as a "yes", then?' asked Toby, laughing.

'I think you probably could.'

'I'll provide the food,' he said. 'Just bring yourselves. Shall we say four-ish?'

'Perfect.'

Fleur and the girls waved Toby off, and shortly afterwards a rather pink-skinned Benjamin came clattering downstairs, followed by his harassed-looking mother.

'Where did you find a change of clothes for him?' asked Fleur.

'Oh, I always take two complete changes with me – you'd be surprised how often they're needed,' said Tilly.

'So you've got another set?'

'Yes, though I'm not planning to need it.'

Fleur explained how she'd accepted Toby's invitation to picnic in his garden. 'He might get grass stains on his trousers or something.'

'Grass stains I can cope with,' said Tilly.

'Genny and I can watch him, Mummy,' said Amelie.

'Really, darling? That's very kind.'

A thump and a yelp from the living room sent them running in to investigate. Benjamin had knocked over a high-back wooden rocking chair and was lying on the floor, with the chair on top of him, pinning him to the floor.

'We could just leave him like that,' said Amelie. 'He can't do anything bad while he's trapped.'

'Shame how tempting that is,' murmured Tilly, as she lifted the chair and attempted to soothe the screaming child.

Somehow, they got through the afternoon with no further accidents, until a knock on the door announced that Toby had returned. He dismissed the idea that they needed to bring any supplies:

'No, I'm providing everything – you're my guests,' he insisted. 'Now, if you're all ready, let's go.' This time, Hattie was allowed to come with them, and she ran ahead, stopping frequently to bark impatiently, clearly directing them all to keep up. Toby allowed Amelie to open the sweet little gate that connected the two gardens, and they all traipsed through.

Dougie the wolfhound was waiting on the other side. He and Hattie ran off at once as if they were old friends.

'Now, don't come back covered in mud!' Fleur shouted after her.

'Does she often get covered in mud?' her sister asked.

'Only when we're meeting Toby,' said Fleur.

'It was only the once,' said Toby, magnanimously. 'And I overreacted horribly.'

'You were in your smart work clothes,' said Fleur.

Tilly looked from one of them to the other, and Fleur felt she could hear her sister telepathically, saying, *Do I sense chemistry between you two?* Luckily, Genevieve tugged on her mother's hand and said,

'Mummy, are we going to have the picnic?'

'Quite right,' said Toby, 'We must get our priorities right. Food before chat, every time.'

He led them to the apple orchard, which he had inherited with the mill. The trees were so old that their trunks were gnarled and their bark covered in lichen. Several picnic rugs had been spread on the ground, and an array of covered dishes was spread on these. Toby removed their covers with a flourish. There were sandwiches in a variety of flavours – including jam – and there were jam tarts and chocolate biscuits.

'Come, eat, eat,' Toby directed them. 'It's lovely and cool here, in the shade.'

He was right: the air was delightfully fresh in this spot beneath the apple trees.

They all tucked in, and Benjamin only smeared jam on himself, the picnic rug, and his mother's skirt – a feat of minimalism which she pronounced 'a miracle'.

After the picnic, Genevieve and Amelie took Benjamin off for a tour of the garden. Hattie and Dougie came running to join them.

'Horsey! Horsey!' shouted Benjamin. He tried to climb on the wolfhound's back.

'No, darling, it's not a horse,' said his mother. 'This is Dougie – he's a dog.'

'No: horsey!' said Benjamin. He tried again to get on to Dougie's back. His sisters had to physically restrain him, holding him around the waist. The dog stood patiently, like a faithful mount.

'He's very good with children,' observed Tilly.

'Yes,' agreed Toby. 'I got him from the dog rescue place. The family he was with before had lots of kids, apparently.'

They found it too expensive to feed him as well as all the children, so eventually, they had to give him up.'

'That's sad,' said Fleur. 'It explains why he's so patient with Benjamin, though.'

They watched the children wander off, one dog on either side of the little party. Then Tilly and Fleur sat back, cradling glasses of Toby's homemade fruit punch, and enjoying the peace and quiet.

'I could get used to this,' said Fleur. She caught Toby's eye and blushed. 'I mean, I could get used to having picnics in the sunshine…'

'You'll have to come again,' said Toby. He stretched out his long legs and leant back against a tree trunk.

A little later, the girls brought a sleepy Benjamin back to the orchard, where he fell asleep with his head in his mother's lap. Dougie stretched out close by and watched over him while Hattie followed the girls on another tour of the garden.

'They'd make very good nannies,' commented Tilly. 'The dogs, I mean.'

'Cheap, too,' agreed Fleur. 'They'd only ask for a bowl of dog food and the occasional chew.' She glanced at Toby and realised he'd been watching her. She looked quickly away, unsure how to interpret his scrutiny.

'I took the wedding dress in, by the way,' he told them. 'The owner thinks he can get the paint out without damaging the dress.'

'Oh, that's fantastic,' said Tilly. 'Thank you so much. I was sure my demon-child had damaged it beyond repair.'

'He's not a demon-child,' said Toby. 'He's just enthusiastic.'

Tilly laughed. 'That's one word for it.' She checked her watch. 'I suppose we should get back fairly soon – I have to get the kids home tonight.'

'What time's Robert due back?' Fleur asked.

'His plane's due in around seven-thirty, so he's hoping to be home by ten. I'd like to have the kids in bed long before then. Not that Benjamin will sleep much tonight, after such a long nap…'

They took their leave soon afterwards, rounding up the reluctant girls, who had an equally reluctant Hattie trailing behind them.

'It's been really lovely,' Tilly told Toby. 'You and Fleur should do it again soon.'

'If Fleur would like to…' said Toby. He looked at Fleur, and she felt herself blush yet again.

'Sorry about my sister,' said Fleur. 'She thinks it's her job to issue invitations on other people's behalf.'

'I don't mind,' said Toby. He took her hand for a moment, and she felt the warmth of it after the cool of the orchard. 'Remember – if you need anything, I'm only next door.'

Tilly repeated this phrase to Fleur later, as she took her farewell. The kids had changed into their pyjamas and had been strapped into their car seats, and Tilly had come back to tell Fleur they were ready to go. She took Fleur's hand and gazed meaningfully into her eyes,

'Remember – if you need anything, I'm only next door,' she said, in a deep voice.

Fleur laughed and pulled her hand away. 'What are you talking about?'

'Toby – he likes you.'

'He's just being friendly because he's new to the area and doesn't know anyone.'

Tilly rolled her eyes. 'He likes you, and he's not just being friendly – he really likes you.'

'Don't say that! I won't be able to talk to him if I think he's not just being neighbourly.'

'You like him too, don't you?'

Fleur went quiet. She felt her cheeks flush.

'I thought so,' said Tilly. She gave Fleur a big hug. 'I love you. Take care of yourself.'

Fleur followed her outside and stood waving as the car headed off down the driveway. Hattie raced the car partway, and then gave up and came back to sniff around the roses that grew close to the house. Fleur fetched her sketchbook and black pen from indoors, and placed a chair on the doorstep, from where she drew little pen-and-ink sketches of Hattie sniffing her way around the garden. Occasionally, thoughts of Toby – his dark eyes and broad shoulders – flashed into her head. These, she wiped away with a deft movement, like an artist rubbing out a pencilled error.

Chapter Eleven

El-Gaish Road
Alexandria
Egypt
28 July, 1928

My dear, sweet silly Alice,

How could you think, even for a moment, that I might have failed to notice you at the ball? I couldn't decide whether to weep or laugh aloud at that suggestion! I love you, my darling: had you worn a black dress with a high collar and boots, I would still have noticed your unique joie de vivre, and that beautiful smile – and I would still have known you were the woman of my dreams. As if Suzanne (delightful though your friend is) could ever have seemed made for me, in the way that you so clearly are!

You are right, of course – Destiny has played more than a small part in our meeting: I am sure of it. We were designed to fit together, just as that small hand you mentioned fits so perfectly inside my own.

I keep reminding myself that your mother and father will accompany you on the voyage. That is a comforting thought, indeed. I would hate to think of your travelling so far, unaccompanied. Once all the excitement of the wedding ceremony is over, however, I must admit that I look forward to beginning our life together, just the two of us, in married bliss.

I am making good contacts here – mainly the owners of private garages, who are keen to acquire the parts to repair the various models that General Motors sells over here. The staff are excellent: Freddie, my deputy, whom I mentioned to you before, has hired only the most trustworthy, experienced sales and distribution staff to support our operation.

I enjoyed another meal at the house of a hospitable local last night, my love. This time, the invitation was courtesy of our chief distribution man: a charming, intelligent man named Farouk Mohamed. Freddie and my neighbour both briefed me beforehand on the correct attire and behaviour. I sat on a bench at a table surrounded by Mr. Mohamed's family: it seems to be the custom for whole generations to live together here in Egypt. I was fed a grain that is known as 'couscous'. It was delicious, especially when doused with a stew-like mix of vegetables and meat. Apparently, this dish hails from North Africa. How I am becoming a man of the world!

Write soon, my darling. It will not be so very long before you are on-board the ship that will bring you to me. How I love that ship, knowing how precious the cargo it will be carrying.

Your impatient fiancé,

Henry

***

1927

Despite the earliness of the hour, the International Motor Exhibition at Olympia was already crowded. Throngs of men were clustered around the stands, talking quickly and excitedly about shafts and chassis.

'It sounds more like an aviation show,' Henry said to his boss.

'I know – all this *torque* and *thrust* business.' Faraday removed a smoking cigar from his mouth and ground it out beneath his shoe. The smell hung around him, a cloud of smoky musk. Henry was finally getting used to the smell, and it now seemed familiar and reassuring, like the scent of mothballs and lavender in his grandmother's cottage in Yorkshire.

'Right,' said Faraday. 'Time to get to business. First, let's check out the competition.'

They headed over to the Lancia stand. The main display was of a 'Lambda' sports car. Flashbulbs went off as newspapermen snapped the vehicle for their papers. Henry and his boss had to wait a while before they could get close.

'Is this the sort of thing you think we should be aiming for with "The Dash"?' asked Faraday.

'Well, it does solve the problem of how to combine the comfort of a saloon interior with the body of a sports car,' said Henry. 'However, I don't think it's relevant to us. It's still a sports car at heart. I see "The Dash" as more of a hybrid car – with space for suitcases for weekends away, and with a sporty appearance without the speeds.'

They continued on, taking in the stands of Bamford Martin and Mercedes before Faraday consulted his brochure. 'GM should be just over there,' he pointed to a stand that was surrounded by visitors. 'Come on – there's someone I want you to meet.'

'Johnny, hi!' A stylish man with greased-back hair and a neat moustache came out from behind the GM stand and shook Faraday's hand. 'And is this the protégé I've heard so much about?'

Henry shook the man's hand. 'I shouldn't think so,' he said, just as Faraday said,

'This is the one. Henry Pemberton, I'd like you to meet Sebastian Locksworth, GM's all-singing, all-dancing Head of Export Sales.'

'Oh, I've heard about you!' said Henry. 'Didn't you come up with the new shipping methods, that saved the company thousands?'

'Guilty as charged.' He smiled at Henry. Then he turned to Faraday. 'Seen anything here I should worry about? I can't get away from the stand for a proper look at our competitors.'

'We've only just got here. I'll catch up with you later, and fill you in. Meanwhile, do you have the new Chevy on display?'

'No such luck. Even I can't get my hands on one – the Americans are keeping her close to their chests at the moment.'

'Maybe next year,' said Faraday.

They said their goodbyes and took up the tour again, taking in new-style hoods and gleaming bonnets. Eventually, they headed over to the Harpenden stand, where their own sales team – a glamorous young blond woman, and a sleek-headed young man – were charming all comers.

Faraday greeted them, 'Gail, Vinnie – you know Henry.'

'Hello, Sirs,' said the sales duo.

'How's it going?' asked Faraday.

Gail pulled out an order book. 'We have around forty orders so far.'

Faraday checked his watch. 'Not bad for eleven-thirty in the morning. Keep up the good work. Got any unusual requests?'

'There's a woman with five little dogs, who wants special seats put in,' said Vinnie.

'Humour her,' instructed Faraday. 'We need to build our reputation for catering to individual tastes.'

'Right, Sir, will do,' said Vinnie. 'And a garage owner from South Kensington came by – said he might be interested in stocking three or four of the Tourers, plus a single "Queenie".'

'Great. Did you get his details?' Gail rummaged through a sheaf of papers and passed a page to Faraday. He scanned the information. 'I'll give him a call later. Let me know if he passes by here again, would you? You can get the venue staff to put out a call for me.'

'Right, Sir – will do,' said Vinnie again.

A middle-aged couple came by, and Faraday and Henry moved off, to give Gail and Vinnie space to attend to their potential clients.

'Good team, those two,' said Faraday, gesturing towards Vinnie and Gail with a cigar he'd just taken from his pocket. He lit it and blew a large gust of smoke from the corner of his mouth. 'Could sell snow to the Eskimos.'

'It would be nice to push a few of "The Dash" and "The Curve", in advance of their release,' said Henry.

Faraday puffed thoughtfully on his cigar for a few moments. 'It's a bit premature. If you're worrying your idea won't sell, stop fretting. The directors never do anything without a thorough check of the market. Plus, we're a British manufacturer, and many people like to buy British.'

Henry remembered hearing Alice talk about the Debonair hat business. Mrs. De Bonneville prided herself on producing her hats in British factories. He also remembered the blue cloche Alice had worn on their last outing – the trip on the Serpentine – and smiled as he recalled the way it had highlighted the perfect green of her eyes.

Faraday took the cigar from his mouth. 'What's going on?' he asked. 'Are you pining for some young filly?'

Henry considered refusing to answer, but he was too besotted – he wanted to proclaim his love from the bonnet of the nearest car.

'Yes, Sir, I am.'

'Who's the lucky girl, then?'

'Her name is Alice De Bonneville.'

'De Bonneville, De Bonneville …' Faraday scrunched up his face in thought. 'Ah – the Debonair hat people?'

'That's right – they are her parents.'

'Pretty girl, if I remember rightly…'

'Very pretty, Sir.'

'Well, do me a favour and marry her quickly. There's nothing more distracting in the workplace than a mooning lover.'

Henry laughed. 'I'll bear that in mind, Sir.'

'Right: let's do another tour of the place before we leave – there are a few designers I'd like to meet with, plus a salesman or two I wouldn't mind poaching. Then we can follow up tomorrow with some of the stands we didn't take in today – I don't remember seeing the Cadillac stand, and there was that large crowd blocking the Studebaker display. '

They headed back towards the main entrance, and Henry had time to think about Alice: how good it had felt to have her arm linked through his, during their walk in Green Park

– and how soft her lips had felt, in that too-short kiss. He had wanted to kiss her passionately and not let her go – but he had held back, out of respect, and because he had been afraid of scaring her off. Part of him still wondered if she might have let him go on kissing her.

They reached a gathering of important-looking men, with gold watch chains showing in their waistcoats.

'The men with the wallets,' Faraday murmured, out of the corner of his mouth. 'Be charming.'

Henry put on his brightest smile and switched off all thoughts of Alice De Bonneville: it was time to do business.

***

'So, when am I to meet this Henry?' Alice's mother glanced up from her book. 'What happened to your weekend date with him?'

'Henry who?' asked Alice's father. He was fiddling with the dials on the huge wireless that stood next to the window. This fine radio set was his pride and joy.

Alice's mother removed her spectacles. 'You know the boy who called for Alice the other week.'

'That doesn't narrow it down much. Ah: Tchaikovsky!' The quaver of a violin emerged from the static of the radio. Alice's father turned to the room with a proud smile.

'Does it need to be that loud?' asked his wife.

'Sorry, sorry!' He hastily turned another knob, and the noise level decreased slightly.

'You know the one,' continued his wife. 'Pemberton. He had the car with the fold-down hood-thing you liked so much.'

'Oh, the chap with the green Austin Seven – yes, of course.'

'He works for the Harpenden Motor Company at Luton,' said Alice, putting down her crocheting. She hated crochet work, but her mother seemed to think it would somehow improve her. The piece she was currently working had started out as a beret but was now beginning to resemble a doily, or perhaps an antimacassar. Her mother had several of her daughter's misshapen crochet pieces, which she used to decorate the back of the sofa and armchairs, much to Alice's chagrin. 'Alice made this,' her mother would announce with pride, to anyone who would listen.

She tuned back into her parents' conversation.

'Seemed like a nice enough chap,' her father was saying. 'Keeps his car in tiptop condition…'

'…Yes, so you said, darling. But I don't think we can judge the quality of a young man by the quality of his car.'

'No, perhaps you're right, my love.' He turned towards Alice. 'So, young lady, what can you tell us about this Henry fellow? Is he a keeper?'

Once again, Alice felt herself blush when asked about Henry. 'Er… He's very nice.'

'Very nice, is he?' asked her father. 'That's high praise from you. I seem to remember one previous beau being written off as "puppy-like".'

'And another was "too entitled", whatever that means,' agreed her mother.

Alice smiled at her parents. 'I haven't spent very long with him, but he acts like a proper grown-up. And he is very kind and thoughtful.'

Her mother nodded. 'So, do you have a date to see him again?'

'Actually, I'm seeing him tonight. He wasn't able to make the weekend after all, and asked if I could go out tonight instead.'

'Why couldn't he make the weekend?' asked her mother – rather sharply, Alice felt.

She laughed. 'I don't think he has a string of girls he's taking out, Mummy – he just had to attend the Motor Exhibition with his boss.'

'I see. What time is he coming?' her mother asked.

'Seven.'

'Very good. We'll have Harris set up tea in the parlour.'

Alice was appalled: she had been looking forward to having Henry to herself.

'Oh no, Mummy – it will be far too late for tea!'

'Nonsense: it's never too late for tea. The two of you will have plenty of time for going out afterwards. Where is he taking you?'

'The Serpentine: he wants to take me out in a boat.'

'Out in a boat, on the Serpentine, in the night? You'll catch your death.'

'Oh Mummy, you know I'm hardy as anything. And I do love boating.'

Her father broke in: 'It won't get dark until at least ten, Christine. And there will be plenty of people around at that hour; it's a very popular spot.'

'I think we should ask your cousin Monty to chaperone,' her mother said.

'Now, now,' said her father. 'Alice is a sensible girl, and this Henry seems trustworthy enough. He got her back as instructed last time.'

'Well, I want to meet him,' said her mother stubbornly.

'Of course, Mummy. I'll have him come in for a few minutes – but not for tea.' Alice's voice was pleading. 'It will get so late.'

Her mother sighed. 'The two of you are too much for me,' she told them, picking up her book from her lap and putting her glasses back on.

Alice exchanged a grin with her father – she could always count on him to take her side.

***

Henry was sure he heard a squeal from inside the house when he rang the doorbell just before seven that evening. He'd spent the past twenty minutes driving around the area, having been so excited about seeing Alice De Bonneville that he'd arrived far too early.

The door was opened by a maid, who showed him through to the parlour. Alice's father and mother stood up to greet him as he entered.

'Henry, good to see you,' said her father. 'This is my wife, Christine.'

'Good evening, Sir. Pleased to meet you, Madam.' Henry shook Mrs. De. Bonneville's hand, and was aware of her gaze, scrutinising him. She gestured for him to take a seat.

'So – how's that car of yours?' Mr. De. Bonneville asked as Henry sat down in one of the formal brocade armchairs.

'Very nice, thank you, Sir. She runs like a dream.'

'Glad to hear it. I always did like those Austin Sevens. What about Harpenden – are they good to work for?'

'Very good, Sir. I work for Johnny Faraday in Sales. Do you know him?'

'Faraday… I know the name, all right. I don't think I've met the gentleman himself.'

'So, I believe you're taking Alice boating,' said Mrs. De Bonneville.

Her husband broke in: 'I always did like a bit of boating. Took Christine here out a number of times, I seem to remember.'

'Just the once, dear,' said his wife quietly. 'And I lost my hat.'

'No shortage of hats now, though, is there?' her husband guffawed. 'Alice shouldn't be long, Henry. Some sort of dress crisis going on upstairs, no doubt.'

'Oh, I hope not on my account,' said Henry. 'She's so beautiful, I'd hate to think of her going to any trouble...' He trailed off, as he realised he was enthusing a little too much in front of her parents. 'I mean...'

'You've got it bad, young man, haven't you? Well, I'll tell you: you're not the first,' said Alice's father, with a grin.

'Oh...' Henry felt as if her father had punched him in the ribcage.

'Thomas – really!' Alice's mother reprimanded her husband. She was a formally dressed lady, the narrow waist of her silhouette suggesting she wore a traditional corset beneath her clothes. She had fine bone structure and glossy hair, which she wore pinned up. She looked a little like Alice, though without the mischievous sparkle in her eyes.

'It's all right,' said Alice's father. 'He's her favourite so far, from what I can tell.'

'Thomas!' said his wife again. She turned to Henry. 'You must excuse him, Mr...'

'...Pemberton,' said Henry.

'Oh, of course – you're Virginia Pemberton's niece, aren't you? Alice did mention it. All of us in the WI were so fond of your aunt. She is a real loss.'

'Thank you.'

'Are your parents still alive?'

'Yes. They live in Cheshire, so I don't see them as often as I'd like. My father's ill health means they don't travel much.'

'What a shame.'

'Yes. I used to work for his cloth company, but he felt there was more of a future for me here in the South. He knew how passionate I was about working in the automobile industry.'

They all looked up as Alice almost ran into the room.

Henry stood up.

'I'm so sorry to keep you waiting!' she told him, holding out her hand for him to shake. 'Have Mummy and Daddy been interrogating you horribly?'

'Not at all,' he said, politely.

'Your mother had barely got started,' said Alice's father, drily. 'What was it, Alice? A clothing crisis of some sort? I told Henry it was sure to be something of that ilk.'

Alice looked offended. 'Certainly not. Martha had scraped her elbow, and I was tending to it.'

'Alice, I've told you time and again,' said her mother, 'We have servants to tend to these things.'

'But it was the servant who was injured,' protested Alice.

'Now is perhaps not the time…' said Alice's father, nodding towards their guest.

His wife sighed. 'No, perhaps not. Anyway, the two of you had better get off quickly, or there won't be enough light to see your way.'

'Lost on the Serpentine,' said Alice's father, musingly. 'Doesn't have quite the same thrill to it as "Lost at Sea", does it?'

'I'm hoping no one's going to be lost anywhere,' said Alice's mother, primly.

'Now, remember we're counting on you to look after our daughter,' Mr. De Bonneville told Henry. 'And have her back by eleven o'clock again, all right?'

'Yes, Sir,' said Henry. He had to drag his eyes away from the sight of Alice, radiantly pretty in a blue floral dress that brought out the green of her eyes. Although the dress was quite long, it was tied at the waist and still showed off her lovely, lithe figure.

He held out his arm to Alice, and they walked through the house to the front door. Alice giggled when they had to squeeze close together to pass through the hallway. Alice's father opened the door for them. He peered out at Henry's car.

'You'll have to take me for a drive one of these days,' he told Henry.

'Yes, Sir: it would be a pleasure.'

It was a balmy evening, and the top of the car was down. Henry helped Alice into the passenger's seat, and said,

'I'll just close the roof.'

'Oh no,' protested Alice. 'It will be lovely to feel the breeze as we travel.'

As he walked around to the driver's door, Henry reflected that Alice De Bonneville was not like other young women he had courted. They would have been terrified of messing up their hair – in short, they would be concerned about 'looking a fright' by the time they arrived at their destination. Alice was wearing a hat – a felt cloche, in the same cornflower blue as her dress. Held in place with an enormous hat pin, and with her hair tucked neatly in place, there was nothing really for the wind to mess up. However, he had trouble imagining Alice looking anything other than beautiful: even with her hair dishevelled, she would surely still be exquisite. Her father was right: Henry did 'have it bad' for this slightly unconventional young woman. He was glad that – if their previous walk in the park was anything to go by – she appeared to share his feelings.

He glanced across at his passenger. She was holding on to her pinned-on hat, and grinning, as London's landscape unfolded before her.

'Are you enjoying the ride?' he shouted, above the engine.

'Loving it!' she told him. 'It's such fun.'

'I love you, Alice De Bonneville,' he told her, impulsively.

She glanced across at him, clearly shocked, and he wished for a moment that he could take it back. Why had he said out loud what he was thinking? It wasn't like him to be so spontaneous in expressing his emotions. Now, he felt vulnerable.

There was a pause, during which he was grateful for the loud noise of the tyres on the road and the engine's whirr. Then she said,

'I've never met anyone like you.'

It wasn't as good as hearing she loved him – but it was a start. It was early days, after all. What was he thinking, telling a woman he loved her, after one date? He would have to be more careful from now on – after all, he didn't want to scare her off. Alice was special, and he was determined to do things correctly.

They were soon close to Hyde Park, where he found a spot for his car, and they walked through the Park gates and followed the path to the Serpentine. Despite the lateness of the hour, several of the boats were out on the water, with men rowing and their female companions sitting back, enjoying the cool breeze on this warm night.

'The boat owner took Henry's money and directed the couple to one of the boats. Henry helped Alice into the little wooden vessel, and she sat back and dipped her fingers into the water.

'It's freezing!' she exclaimed.

'Better not fall in then,' said the boat owner over his shoulder as he walked back to his hut.

Henry took the oars and rowed skilfully out into the centre of the lake.

'Isn't it lovely here?' said Alice.

He gazed at her pretty features. 'Beautiful.'

She blushed, and he wondered if he'd gone too far again – she was hard to read. Then she said,

'What is it about you, Henry Pemberton?'

He paused in his rowing. 'What do you mean?'

She met his gaze, and the evening sun lit her hair like an angel's. 'I feel as if you've always been in my life.'

'Is that a good thing?'

'That depends.'

'On what?'

'On whether you're planning to stay in my life.' He saw her flush at her own forwardness.

'Well, that's up to you,' he told her.

'Is it?'

He studied her. There was a delicate tilt to her chin, which suggested both obstinacy and fragility.

He rested the oars in their supports and leaned across, taking both her hands in his.

'You know already that I love you, Alice De Bonneville. Would you do me the honour of becoming my wife? You don't have to decide straight away: I will wait for an answer if you want time to consider it.'

'There's nothing to consider,' she said simply. 'I already feel like we were destined to be together.'

He felt his heart lurch with hope and urgency. 'So…is that a yes?'

'It's a yes,' she said, smiling.

The boat rocked precariously as he reached over to pull her into his arms. The voice of the boat owner came over a loud hailer: 'Will the customers in Boat Number Six please stop rocking the boat?'

Henry and Alice laughed as Henry carefully moved back into position and took up the oars.

'I will have to ask your father,' he said.

'He'll say yes.'

'You sound very sure.'

'He likes your car. He always says you can tell a lot about a man by his choice of car.'

'Well, it looks as though I'll be lucky enough to have my two favourite ladies to keep me company from now on, then.'

'Your two favourite ladies?'

'My Austin Seven – whom I call "Sarah Jane" – and you.'

Chapter Twelve

Fleur was on the phone with her agent. She had been talking for a long time – as testified by a large number of doodles on her phone pad. She inhaled the strong scent of lilies from the bunch she'd placed the day before on the study table. Most of her doodles represented these dramatic pink blooms with their freckled petals. Hattie the Labrador had become bored during the long conversation and was lying beneath the desk, head on paws. Fleur, though, was far from bored. She bounced excitedly in her seat.

'I still can't believe that Bloomsbury is interested,' she said.

Her agent Nicole's voice on the other end of the phone sounded almost as excited.

'It's fantastic news, Fleur – but you have worked hard, so it's well-deserved. They loved *Freddie goes to School* and *Sky Dreaming*. I think they're going to want you to work with someone from their own author lists.'

'That's fine – it's always nice to work with a new writer. I wonder who they'll match me up with.'

'Let's set up that meeting, and you can find out what their plans are.'

Fleur fished beneath her notepad for her diary, and she and Nicole came up with a few potential dates to meet with the editors at the prestigious publishing house.

Just as she put the phone down, the doorbell sounded. Hattie ran to the front door, barking like a guard dog. Fleur skipped after her and threw open the door.

'I might be about to get a publishing deal with a big publisher!' she told the post woman.

'Oh, right,' said the woman, sounding unimpressed. 'My brother-in-law is a writer. His books are in the Amazon Bestseller lists.'

'Oh, I'm an illustrator, rather than a writer.'

'I don't suppose illustrators get much credit,' said the post woman. 'I mean, aren't you just putting pictures to someone else's story?'

'Well, that depends... Often, the illustrator has joint credit with the writer.'

'Hmm,' said the post woman. 'Well, good luck with that.' She turned to leave, and Hattie trotted out to bark at her.

'Sorry,' said Fleur, grabbing Hattie's collar. 'She doesn't normally bark at people...'

'Hmm,' said the post woman again, climbing into her van and turning it too quickly as usual, before roaring off along the drive. Feeling somewhat deflated, Fleur headed into the kitchen, to make some tea.

'I thought it was exciting,' she told the dog, over the sound of the kettle boiling.

Hattie barked once in agreement. Then she started to bark again. She ran out of the kitchen, her feet scrabbling against the hallway's parquet floor.

'I hope it's not the post woman coming back,' said Fleur disconsolately. She trailed after Hattie and was in time to open the door as the bell sounded.

On the doorstep stood Toby. 'Sorry to bother you...' he began. Then he caught her expression. 'Hey – what's wrong?'

'I've got a meeting at Bloomsbury. It looks like they're going to sign me.'

'But that's fantastic!'

'The post woman didn't think so.'

He laughed. 'Really? Are you going by that grumpy woman's response? She only cheers up when somebody dies.'

Feeling a bit better, Fleur said, 'Would you like a cup of tea?'

His face fell. 'Oh... I'd love one, but I've... Well, that's why I'm here, actually: I have to pop over to Worcestershire for a day or two, and it would be so much easier not to take Dougie...'

'We'd love to have him, wouldn't we, girl?' Fleur said to her dog. Hattie barked excitedly, having heard her friend's name.

'That's great. I've got him in the car – sorry, I know it's a bit presumptuous...'

'It's fine. Let him out, and I'll take them both for a walk.'

'Thanks so much. I will make it up to you.' He opened the car door, and Dougie jumped neatly down, running to greet Hattie. 'So, how about dinner, when I get back, to thank you?' said Toby.

Fleur remembered her sister's theory that Toby had feelings for her. She tried – and failed – not to blush.

'Yes, dinner would be nice,' she mumbled.

'Only if you want to,' he insisted. She looked up at him. His dark eyes were grave. She swallowed down her awkwardness and made herself smile at him.

'I'd love to,' she said.

'That's a date then,' he said and walked back to his Land Rover before she had time to question what kind of 'date' he meant.

Chapter 13

22 Beaumont Street

London

14 August, 1928

My dear Henry,

I am so excited to hear of how things progress with your new job. I am exceedingly proud of my clever, talented, courageous husband. Not many men would have dared to commit to so bold a move to foreign climes.

Will you take me to see your offices, once I am in Alexandria? I want to see whether the images I have formed, of Mr Mohamed and 'Freddie', are at all like their originals. I want to see if the place is at all like the ornately tiled building I have in my head (I may have taken out too many books from the library, on Arabic architecture).

Henry, what will I do with my time, when you are at work? Do you think I should take a job myself? I can type a little... and transcribe – I have neat writing, do I not? (Is this really the sum of my talents? How paltry they appear!)

You did make me smile, with your insistence that you would still have noticed me at the Palmsworth ball, even had I worn a high-neck dress and boots! How blind you have become, since falling in love. However, I shall overlook this – and any other – weakness, which pays me such a compliment.

Do you remember your proposal, in the boat at Hyde Park? I am sure you do. I blush every time I recall it: how I very nearly proposed to you, instead! I feel quite ashamed when I relive that moment, in 'Boat Number Six'. How forward I was, how indecorous and unladylike! My mother must never find out. My shame swiftly dissolves into laughter, however, when I recall the boat owner's announcing that we were to 'stop rocking the boat'!

I look forward to laughing with you a great deal, once we are living together, as husband and wife.

Yours forever,

Alice

***

1927

Henry was sitting in the office with his boss, discussing the potential to expand Harpenden's export sales.

'Take Egypt, for example,' Henry said. 'The market is waiting for a luxury vehicle.'

'Egypt, you say? That's quite a coincidence,' said Johnny, stubbing out his cigar. 'Look, I have a proposition for you, but I'm not sure what you'll make of it…'

Henry sat up straight at his desk. 'Go on.'

'I've heard General Motors is looking for a Parts Manager for its new Alexandrian office.'

'Are you firing me?'

Faraday laughed. 'I'm promoting you.'

'You're promoting me by suggesting I move to another company?'

'Henry, I want you to go over there and feedback to us on everything: the state of the market; any openings for Harpenden over there; the things that GM do well and could do better…'

Henry raised an eyebrow at his boss. 'You want me to be your spy?'

'I'd rather you thought of it as being our advance party.'

'I see. And what if GM doesn't want me for the job?'

Faraday swatted away the problem. 'The position's yours if you want it. My friend Seb Locksworth took a shine to you at the Motor Exhibition.'

'As in GM's head of export sales?'

'That's the one. So, what do you say?'

'Can I think about it?'

'Of course. But don't take too long – it's a pretty attractive job offer. You'll receive a pay rise, and even your own car.'

'My own car?'

'That's right. I've heard they're handing out free cars like sweets at the moment.'

Henry thought about his own car – a 1925 Austin Seven. He loved his racing-green convertible, 'Sarah Jane' – but she needed frequent work to keep her in good running order. The thought of a brand-new car was certainly appealing.

'I'll give it some thought,' he said at last.

'You do that,' said Faraday, lighting his next cigar. The office was once again becoming hazy from the smoke. Henry threw open a window and gulped in some damp, rather grimy Luton air. Perhaps he'd soon be basking in the Egyptian sunshine.

***

The following morning – after a virtually sleepless night –
Henry was already at his desk when his boss arrived.

'Have you given some thought to my proposition?'
Faraday asked as he hung up his hat and coat.

'I have – and it's a "yes".'

'Well, that's good. Be sorry to lose you here, mind –
but I could do with a reliable set of ears and eyes over in
Alexandria. I'll give Sebs a call this morning – he'll be
relieved to have someone he knows.'

'Does he also know that you're planning to have me spy
on his operations on your behalf?'

Faraday paused on his way to his desk. 'Oh, not that word
again. Let's not call it "spying" – more like researching the
market and feeding information back.'

'All right: does Mr Locksworth know that I'll be feeding
information back to you?'

'Not exactly. But he's no idiot: he knows you're my man.'

'So I don't have to use carrier pigeons and coded
telegrams?'

'Don't sound so disappointed. You can send me coded
telegrams if it helps.'

Faraday made the call. Then he put down the receiver and
said,

'Sebs is delighted to have you onboard. So now all you
need is a companion.'

'A companion?'

'Of course – be a bit lonely out there for you, new country
and all. Have you asked that Debonair hat girl to marry you
yet?' Faraday leaned back and puffed on his cigar. The fug of
smoke around him gave him the air of a mystical wise man,
shrouded in mist.

'I have.'

'Did she say yes?'

'She did. However, I still need to ask her father.'

'Just a formality, I'm sure.'

'I hope so, Sir.' Henry brightened: 'He likes my car, at least.'

'So, both father and daughter have taste,' said Faraday, making Henry blush. 'I'm sure it will all be fine. You've been so distracted lately, you've obviously got it bad. Go over there tonight, why don't you? Get it over with.'

'Maybe I should,' said Henry, feeling his stomach clench at the thought. What if Mr De Bonneville said no? He couldn't bear it. All of his happiness was bound up in Alice – in marrying her, and living with her for the rest of his life. He couldn't stop thinking about her – the way she frowned when she was thinking; the way she threw back her head and laughed… He had it bad, all right.

'I'll get on to asking her father, as soon as I get the chance.'

'Good, good… Oh, and Henry?'

'Yes?'

'Get her family to make you a present of a new hat – the one you wear at the moment looks downright foolish.'

Henry marvelled at how many of his conversations with his boss involved holding his tongue. This time, he managed not to tell Johnny Faraday that, whilst Henry's fedora was the height of fashion, Faraday's battered flat cap was the one that could do with being replaced.

Would Alice still want to marry him, if it meant starting a new life overseas, far from her family and friends? He decided that he would go over to her house later – first to see her, and then, if she was still to be his bride, to see her father. He watched the clock to such an extent, that Faraday noticed.

'What is going on?' he asked, at last. 'You're as twitchy as a dog with fleas. You're driving me mad.'

'Sorry, Johnny.'

'Is it this Alice girl?'

'Yes…'

'You're worried she won't want you if there's an emigration on the cards?'

'That about sums it up.'

'Go now,' said Faraday.

'Excuse me?'

'I can't work with you in this state – and you can't get anything done. Just take the afternoon off, and go over there now. Ask the girl, then ask her father – and come in tomorrow, happy but calmer.'

Henry didn't wait to be told again. He grabbed his jacket from the back of the chair. At the door, he paused:

'Thanks, Johnny. I'll be better tomorrow, I promise' … *whatever the outcome*, he said to himself, under his breath.

Henry slowed as he approached the De Bonnevilles' tall townhouse in his Austin Seven. He should have rung to alert them. It was terribly rude to turn up like this, unannounced and uninvited. As he stopped in front of the house and hesitated, the front door flew open and Alice came running down the steps, smoothing her hair beneath a burgundy felt hat. It was damp out, and she had on a dark-red woollen coat and red boots. Henry felt a surge of tenderness upon seeing her. There was something vulnerable in the way her hands kept pushing her hair beneath the hat, attempting to subdue it. She spotted him, sitting in his car, and walked over. He climbed out before she reached him.

'Hello,' she said, 'were we expecting you?'

'No, I'm sorry – I just had to see you about something. I should have called first. I can see you're busy.'

'I'm meeting Mummy at my aunt's. Will you walk with me? It isn't far – just Walden Road. It's only about five minutes from here.'

'Of course.' He offered her his arm, and they began to walk.

'So, what was it?' asked Alice. 'Have you changed your mind?'

'Changed my…?' She had said it so casually, it took him a moment to comprehend that she was talking about his proposal. 'Oh, no! Nothing like that!'

'That's good then,' she said, with a smile.

'But I do have some news – about my job – and I'm hoping it won't change anything.'

'Go on…'

'Johnny Faraday – my boss – has fixed me up with a job working for General Motors in Egypt.'

She stopped walking abruptly and turned to look at him. 'Egypt?'

'Yes. It's… I…'

'Is it a more senior role?'

'In a way. It's certainly better pay. I'd be Parts Manager over there.'

'I don't fully understand. You work for Harpenden at the moment…'

'Yes, but Mr Faraday has a good friend who's high up at GM and this friend wants me for the job. Mr Faraday thinks it will be a good opportunity for us to size up the market in Egypt.'

She turned to begin walking again. 'In that case, it's a fantastic opportunity, and you must take it.'

'But…Alice.' He drew her to a standstill again and turned her gently to face him. 'How do you feel about it? Would you still be my wife?'

She gazed up at him. 'Of course I would. We've already agreed to all that, haven't we?'

He loved her even more for the nonchalant way in which she said this – as if nothing mattered, so long as they were together.

'I have to ask your father, of course.'

'He's back at the house now. Why don't you take me to my aunt's and then go back to the house, to see him?'

'Are you sure I won't be intruding?'

'He won't mind. After all, he'll be getting rid of me, which can only be a good thing, I should think.'

This seemed highly unlikely to Henry: he couldn't imagine anyone's considering Alice as anything other than precious.

They hadn't walked far before Alice said,

'Here we are – the house with the green door.'

'Shall I say goodbye here, then?'

'Oh, no – you must come in and meet my cousins.'

'Must I?' Henry felt mildly alarmed, at this new development.

'I want everyone to see what a handsome husband I'm going to have.'

'But you haven't told them yet about the engagement…?'

She flashed him a charming smile. 'Well, I might have whispered something to my cousins, Louisa and Francesca. No one else knows, though, so don't give the game away, will you?'

Feeling even more nervous, Henry escorted Alice into the house, where he was greeted most civilly by a house full of women – or so it appeared. There were Alice's mother, Alice's aunt, and the aunt's daughters, Louisa and Francesca, who never seemed to stop talking. Their mother continually reprimanded them, but they paid no attention. They gathered around Alice's chair and kept firing questions at both her and Henry.

'Uncle Thomas said you have a very nice car,' said Francesca, the younger of the two. She was about sixteen, Henry guessed and she had a sweet, open expression, which made him like her at once.

'That's very kind of your Uncle Thomas,' he told her. 'She's a couple of years old now but she's still lovely to drive.'

'Will you take us for a ride in it?'

'Francesca!' her sister scolded, shocked. 'You can't ask things like that – we've only just met him.' Louisa was around eighteen though she had a confidence and grace which meant that her fashionable clothing gave her an air older than her years.

'I would love to take you for a drive if your mother and father would care to accompany us,' said Henry. And perhaps your cousin Alice, too.' He smiled at Alice and felt the now familiar lurch of his heart as she smiled back. He marvelled at how strongly he felt for this pretty young woman, with the lovely smile and the sparkle in her eyes.

'And now, if you'll excuse me,' he said, 'I have a rather important meeting to attend.'

Alice's aunt showed him out. 'Good luck,' she said. He looked at her in surprise, and she winked and added, 'with the very important meeting about which I know nothing…' He decided not to ask her how she knew.

The walk back to Alice's house took too little time. He felt underprepared for this encounter, which – however, it went – was set to change the course of his life. He paused at the foot of the steps to the front door. A light rain was falling, and he turned his face to the sky for a moment, while he mustered his courage. Then he climbed the steps and rang the doorbell.

A manservant opened the door and showed him through to the parlour. Henry paced the room for a few minutes, saying over and over to himself, under his breath, 'I'd like to marry your daughter'. After a few minutes, Mr De Bonneville appeared.

'Henry, good to see you.' They shook hands, and Alice's father gestured for Henry to take a seat in one of the formal brocade armchairs. Once they were both seated, he said, 'What can I do for you?'

Henry took a deep breath and plunged straight in:

'Sir, I would like your permission to marry your daughter.' There was a long pause, and Henry added: 'I mean Alice.'

'I know who my daughter is.' Mr De Bonneville whistled softly and leaned back in his chair, stretching out his legs. 'Well, you've caught me somewhat on the hop, I must say.'

'I'm sorry, Sir. I may have to go abroad soon for work, and I wanted to finalise everything beforehand.'

'How long are you travelling for?'

'It's indefinite. If the arrangements go through, I'll be heading up the parts sales division for General Motors in Alexandria.'

'So you're proposing to whisk my daughter off to Egypt?'

'Yes, Sir…'

Mr De Bonneville went quiet. At last, he tucked in his legs and sat forward.

'What did Alice say? I'm assuming you asked her before you came to me?'

'I did, Sir. She said yes.'

'Even to the move to Alexandria?'

'She has agreed to come with me to Egypt.'

'I see… And you two have known each other how long…?'

'A few weeks, Sir.'

'Is this normal, for you, to propose marriage to a girl after just a few weeks? Are you always so impulsive?'

'No, Sir. In fact, I've never proposed before.'

'Glad to hear that, at least.'

There was another long pause. Henry's anxiety crept up; he could feel his shirt sticking to his back. He watched Mr De Bonneville closely, desperate for some sign as to whether the outcome would go his favour.

'Is the rush purely down to the fact that you are moving overseas?' asked Mr De Bonneville at last.

Henry shook his head. 'No, Sir. It's…' he sought the right words. '…I've never met anyone like your daughter before, Sir. She…we seem to fit together. When I'm with her, it just feels…right – as if we belong together.' He hadn't meant to gabble like that. He felt himself grow even hotter, with awkwardness and anxiety. Mr De Bonneville was a hard man to read.

There was another pause, and then Mr De Bonneville nodded as if he'd made his decision. He stood up and shook Henry's hand. Henry, still awaiting the verdict, was taken aback. At last, with a strange sense of déjà vu – harking back to his actual proposal to Alice – he said,

'Is that a yes, Sir?'

'It's a yes, young man. But only because Alice has already accepted you, and I trust her taste and judgment.'

Henry stood up and grabbed the hand that had just dropped his own. He pumped it hard. 'Thank you, Mr De Bonneville – thank you so much. I'm going to make Alice so happy.'

'You'd better,' said her father. 'She'll be your responsibility now.' He walked over to the drinks cabinet and poured two brandies. 'Here's to the future happiness of my daughter and son-in-law.'

'Thank you, Sir.' In his relief, Henry drank his brandy too quickly and started coughing. Thomas patted him on the back until the coughing had eased.

'Now, sit back down.'

Henry obediently took his seat again in the armchair.

'We have to work out how to break this to Alice's mother.'

'Will she take it badly, Sir?'

'If we're going to be related, you'd better call me Thomas.' He thought for a moment. 'I think speed, rather than diplomacy, don't you?'

Henry felt poorly placed to judge the best way for Thomas De Bonneville to break any news to his wife: he hardly knew her.

'Won't she be pleased about the marriage? Did she have… something else in mind for Alice?'

'If you mean *someone* else, then no. As to whether she'll be pleased about the marriage, it's hard to know. I think so. She took quite a liking to you, on your brief visit the other evening.'

'So, perhaps it won't be such a terrible announcement after all?'

Thomas laughed, but his laugh had a sardonic undertone. 'Not such a terrible announcement, to tell a mother her only child is emigrating?'

Henry had to admit that Thomas made a good point. However, he himself was too full of happiness to allow the possibility of Christine's disappointment to seep in.

'What sort of time frame are we talking about here?' Thomas asked.

Henry considered. 'I imagine it could all happen quite quickly. I would need to be one of the first out there, to get things moving.'

'I see.'

There was another silence. Henry wondered if he was obliged to stay, to help Thomas to plan the announcement to his wife. He was desperate to leave – to see Alice, and tell her the good news.

'Would you excuse me, Sir, if I headed straight back to Walden Road?' he asked, breaking the silence. 'I'd like to tell Alice.'

Thomas De Bonneville seemed to come out of some reverie. 'Of course – you should head straight over there.' He stood up and walked with Henry to the front door. 'I love that girl,' he told Henry, as they shook hands on the threshold. 'I only hope you prove yourself worthy of her.'

'I will do my utmost to be a good husband to her,' said Henry, looking his future father-in-law in the eye. 'I truly love her, more than I can say.'

Thomas nodded. 'That's all I needed to hear. Now go and see her. But do me a favour – leave it to me to tell her mother.'

Henry almost ran back to Walden Road. He arrived, out of breath and grinning, despite the grey sky and continuous drizzle. As soon as he was shown into the parlour, where the women were still chatting and laughing, he caught Alice's eye and gave a smile and a nod. She at once broke into an enormous smile herself. He hurried over to her, and quietly confirmed the good news.

'But your father wants to be the one to tell your mother, so we must keep it secret for a little while longer,' he whispered.

She nodded up at him and smiled, and he wondered that the whole of London couldn't hear his happiness, singing out like a choir from every fibre of his body.

Chapter Fourteen

A friend of Fleur's mother had kindly come over to mind the dogs for the day, so that Fleur could attend the meeting her agent had scheduled for her, with an editor at Bloomsbury Publishing.

'I miss my old Boris and Lucille, so it will be nice for me to spend some time with dogs again,' Fleur's mother's friend had said, referring to the pair of Chihuahua siblings she'd had for years, but who had died the previous year.

Now, despite the earliness of the hour, this kind lady was already downstairs, and getting ready to take the dogs for a long morning walk, while Fleur examined her reflection in readiness for leaving for London. She had selected her outfit the night before. It comprised a sixties' shift dress by the famous Palm Beach designer Lilly Pulitzer, in a pretty green-floral print, with a matching cropped jacket. On her legs, she wore seamed silk stockings that she'd found in an unopened packet in one of her grandmother's drawers. Her feet proudly bore the snakeskin shoes that she had coveted for so long. She'd even found a matching clutch bag, which she placed beneath her arm. On her head, she wore a neat pillbox hat. The whole look was very 'Jackie O', and she felt chic and confident.

The local taxi driver came five minutes early, and she was ready and waiting for him outside. The air had the hazy, just-woken-up coolness that signals a hot day to come.

'Nice get-up,' said the taxi driver, as she climbed into the back seat. 'My wife says she'd love a wardrobe like yours. Where do you get it all from?'

'It all belonged to my grandmother.'

'She was always a stylish lady. I don't recognise the clothes you wear, though.'

'Grandma Alice had a lot of clothes from previous decades, that she no longer wore. I'm having a lovely time, unearthing them and giving them an airing. She would have laughed if she could see me.'

'She'd have been pleased, though?'

'Oh, yes: she loved to see us dress up in her outfits.'

Fleur remembered that the driver's wife worked at the village bakery. The woman had to wear an unflattering white coat for work, so Fleur had never seen her actual clothing... Except that, now she came to think of it, she had spotted her wearing some kitten-heel peep-toe shoes, with a rosette.

'Oh – your wife has some fabulous shoes,' she said.

He snorted. 'They're completely impractical – I don't know how she gets away with it. The staff are supposed to wear sensible, non-slip soles.'

'I suppose she can't completely deny her inner fashion-consciousness.'

He laughed. 'It must be something like that. She does love those shoes.' He said this fondly, and Fleur imagined a special room filled with racks of beautiful footwear, which he tolerated because they made his wife happy.

The train station and its environs were full of commuters when the taxi pulled in to the car park. Her meeting was at ten o'clock, and she hadn't wanted to take any chances with late-running trains: this appointment was too important to miss.

The train came in bang on cue, and she climbed aboard, among the crowds of besuited office workers. She found herself a seat, at a table by the window. From there, she sat, sketching impressions: first of the Suffolk heathland; then of the Essex fields and hedgerows; and finally of the capital's outskirts: rows of houses flashing past; the occasional tower block; a fox, trotting along with its cubs and vanishing into a large hole in the bank. There were masses of purple and pink lupins – and buddleia, growing out of impossible cracks in concrete walls, or even rooted in heaps of stone. Her mother had called buddleia 'the kamikaze shrub' and it was easy to see why – it would grow anywhere, however daunting or vertigo-inducing the site.

At last, the train pulled in to Liverpool Street Station. As she followed the commuters-on-autopilot out through the ticket gates, a musical birdsong from the rafters caused her to pull up short. It was a male blackbird. She passed through the gates, then took up a spot in the centre of the station, where she wouldn't be in anyone's way. She looked around until she spotted him: a small, dark silhouette against the high roof. As other people walked on, oblivious, Fleur watched him and listened to the perfect pitch of his serenade. It was exquisite. When he eventually flew off, she headed out to the street, to catch a bus to the town centre. She felt as though his song had left an imprint on her: a promise of something lovely and rare.

Chapter Fifteen

El-Gaish Road

Alexandria

Egypt

23 August, 1928

My dear Alice,

Of course, I shall take you to visit the office: I shall be showing you off at every opportunity, and that is too good a one to miss. Mr. Mohamed and his wife have kindly expressed a great interest in meeting you – and I know you will enjoy Freddie's good humour and keen brain. Mr. Mohamed's wife, Fatima, has volunteered to be your guide, to the area as well as the social customs. She is as charming as her husband, and I feel sure you will enjoy her company.

If you wish to work, then I shall not be the one to stand in your way. However, I think you will find there is quite enough to occupy you, here. There are groups of women, into whose midsts you will, I know, be welcomed. There is an interesting mix here, of the local women with the expatriates. I believe, with your natural curiosity for other people and their ways, that you will find the crossing of cultures quite fascinating. Perhaps you might write a book, delving into the sociological aspects of this.

You need never blush, recalling that proposal, my darling: I have heard that proposing is a terrifying prospect for most men. You, however, made it the easiest, least daunting process in the world. I look forward to 'rocking the boat' with you for the rest of our lives together.

I must finish now if I am to have time to look over the books before bed. Know that I would far rather spend the time with you…

Your devoted, soon-to-be husband,

Henry

***

1928

'I have a treat for you, Alice.'

'What is it, Mummy?'

'I thought we could go shopping for your trousseau tomorrow.'

Alice put down her book. It was very thick and she was having trouble getting into it – there were too many characters, and her head was too full of her impending marriage to keep track of their names.

'Don't you need to work?' she asked.

'Mr. Francis can easily deal with any problems at the store in my absence. I had been intending to do some stock-taking at the warehouse, but I think the girls there can manage without me.'

'A real shopping outing?' Alice was already envisaging the sort of clothes she'd like to take with her to Egypt, to start her married life – chiffon dresses with braiding or embroidery, with pale leather shoes and matching handbags.

'I thought we'd head to Bond Street,' said her mother. 'There are some lovely little boutiques there, and Fenwick department store.'

Alice's heart sank. 'It's a bit fuddy-duddy,' she said.

'Well, where would you rather go?' asked her mother. 'You will be a wife now, you know – you have a respectable appearance to maintain.'

'How about Selfridges?' asked Alice.

Her mother seemed doubtful. 'It's not at the better end of Oxford Street, darling. And I do prefer Bond Street. Plus, that rather strange American man owns Selfridges, and I've never quite trusted him – there's something far too...liberal about him.'

'Please, Mummy! They have some gorgeous dresses and a simply divine Chinese coat I've had my eye on for ages.'

'All right,' conceded her mother. 'But if we don't find anything I consider suitable, we shall have to try elsewhere.'

'Thank you, Mummy!' Alice threw her arms around her mother and kissed her on the cheek. Her mother laughed – she could never resist Alice's effusive gestures.

A short time later, Alice and her mother were stepping out of a black cab by the large front doors of Selfridges department store. They headed inside and took the lift up to the ladies' fashion department, where smiling young women were waiting to tend to their needs.

Indeed, once they understood how large a sum Alice's mother was planning to spend, the sales assistants seemed especially keen to please. Soon, three of them were running backwards and forwards, their arms full of clothes in varying sizes and colours.

'Hmm,' said Alice's mother, looking Alice up and down inside the large changing room. Alice was wearing a dark-blue, knee-length dress with a drop waist and pleated skirt.

On her feet, she wore red patent shoes with a strap. 'The navy suits you very well , especially with the red shoes. But the dress does hang off your slim frame somewhat.'

'That's the fashion, Mummy. You know girls my age aren't wearing corsets.'

Her mother sighed. 'I know, darling – but you have such a pretty figure – it does seem a waste to wear a sack.'

Alice examined the price label. 'Especially such an expensive sack.'

'Would you try a smaller size, at least?'

'Of course, Mummy.'

Her mother nodded to one of the sales assistants, and the young woman ran off to find a smaller size.

'What do you think of the shoes?' Alice asked. 'I think they're rather sweet.'

'They're very nice,' agreed her mother. 'But that's the third pair of shoes we've found. You can't go to Egypt with nothing but footwear.'

Alice laughed. 'It might turn a few heads…'

'Alice, dear, must you be so…'

'…risqué?' suggested Alice. 'I do know how you like that word, Mummy.'

'I only wish I didn't have to apply it to your behaviour or attire quite so often. We didn't bring you up to be so… crude.'

The assistant arrived back with the smaller size, and Alice slipped off the navy dress and drew its replacement over her head.

'Better?' she asked her mother.

'Much better. I think you should take that one.'

'Lovely,' said Alice, admiring her reflection. The navy set off the green of her eyes. She felt a pang of guilt for teasing her mother, who was being so kind. 'You know I'm very well-behaved really, Mummy. I only say those things because you react so wonderfully.'

'Well, I wish you wouldn't.'

'I won't anymore – I shall be the perfect lady.'

'Thank you, my darling. Now, that's one dress. You'll need a lightweight coat to wear over it, but we can choose coats later. We need more dresses.' Her mother beckoned to one of the sales assistants. 'Do you have that floral one we liked, with the buttons?'

'Yes, Madam.' The assistant carefully unfastened the buttons on the sprigged dress, removed it from its hanger and passed it to her. 'Thank you.' She turned to Alice, who was standing in her undergarments. 'Here you are.'

Alice took the dress and slid it over her head. The fabric felt cool against her skin. The dress had a tie belt and a small, white collar. 'Oh, I like this one, Mummy.'

'You'd have to wear a jacket of some kind to cover your shoulders. I think Mrs. Jenkins mentioned something about its being considered indecorous to have bare shoulders.'

'I can have a shawl or something. But isn't it pretty?'

'It is very nice,' her mother agreed. 'I like the way the belt cinches in your waist – it seems a better shape than the navy.'

'Still, if it gets really hot, I'll be glad of some clothes that give me room to breathe.'

'I suppose so. I do wish we had a clearer idea of what you needed, Alice. Henry doesn't seem very knowledgeable on the topic.'

'He knows a lot more than most men would. Don't forget, he's the one who told me to bring a selection of hats, and that we could sort out netting in the mosquito season – he'd been asking the other ladies.'

'That's true…. However, we don't even know what length of the dress is considered appropriate over there. The navy doesn't even quite reach your knees.'

'If you really don't like that one, we don't have to take it, Mummy.'

'Well, shall we see what else there is, and then we can make a decision?'

They were there for hours, trying on dress after dress, and skirt after skirt, together with shoes, gloves, and lightweight coats. Alice's mother was attentive and helpful, offering suggestions on how each outfit might be improved. Her artistic flair was very much in evidence when it came to advising her daughter's sartorial choices.

'I am lucky to have a Mummy like you,' said Alice, affectionately. 'Suzanne's mother won't even go with her to the shops.'

'Really? She'll have to come along with us one of these days…' Her mother trailed off, no doubt realising there wouldn't be much time now, before their departure for Egypt.

'Perhaps you can take her shopping after you get back from Alexandria?' suggested Alice. 'She could be your daughter-substitute.'

'I'm not sure it works like that,' said her mother, laughing. 'You do have some strange ideas!'

'But that's why you love me…' Alice examined her reflection. 'Do you think these coral shoes are a bit too bright, with the pale-pink dress?'

'Possibly. Let's see what else they've got. A pale green might be nice. We have a hat in the new range that would go beautifully.'

'Is it a "traditional lady" hat?' asked Alice.

'No, it's a very modern, up-to-the-minute hat,' said her mother. 'I thought of you as I designed it. Not a speck of brown on it – and no dangling adornments of any description.'

'Then I shall look forward to seeing it.'

Her mother checked her watch. 'I think we'd better get a move on. We haven't found enough clothes for you yet. Now, wasn't there a cream dress-and-coat set in broderie anglaise?'

One of the assistants passed over the embroidered dress and coat. 'Now, I like this,' said her mother approvingly, holding up the hanger. 'It's delicate, without being brazen. You can always wear the coat if it's important to cover up – it's lovely and lightweight.'

Alice wriggled out of the pink dress and handed it to a shop assistant. Then she drew on the cream dress and allowed her mother to help her by fastening the buttons at the back. With the coat over the top, she looked…unlike herself.

'Do you think it's a little "old lady"?' she asked her mother.

'No, I think it perfectly blends the modern with the modest. I imagine it's exactly what you should be wearing, within the expatriate society of Alexandria.'

'I'm just not sure…'

'…I think we should take it,' said her mother. 'The coat might also be useful over your other dresses.' Her mother saw the forlorn look on Alice's face. 'Oh, don't be like that, darling. All right, you choose – but do please bear in mind that you will be representing your country abroad. It's important to show respect for the local customs.'

'I suppose you're right, Mummy. But perhaps I could show my respect with something slightly less bland?'

Mrs. De Bonneville laughed. 'All right, you win – what would you prefer?'

'I liked the embroidered Chinese coat we saw – the red one. And it has sleeves, and comes just below the knee, so it's not disrespectful.'

'Really, darling – red?' her mother sounded doubtful.

'It's so beautiful. And it would look lovely over the navy dress if we decided to take that one…'

The red silk coat was tried on and approved, and added to the large rail of garments that had passed the test. It was another hour, however, before Mrs. De Bonneville felt her daughter had selected enough clothes with which to begin her new life. Even Alice was beginning to flag before her mother declared it time to stop.

When they left, a line of laden shop workers had to follow them out to a waiting taxi. Box after box of dresses, blouses, skirts, gloves, stockings and shoes were piled into the large boot – and more had to be accommodated inside the vehicle.

Once they were safely inside, and the driver had set off, Alice surveyed the boxes at her feet and on the seat beside her. 'Well, Mummy, I think I have enough clothes to live out there forever.'

'Don't be facetious, darling – you know you'll have to come home eventually.'

Alice was silent. She didn't know what the future might hold. Part of her worried that, for all her love of Henry, she might become painfully homesick for London and her parents after a month or two. And what if she and Henry never came home? The thought panicked her – so much so, that she tried not to dwell on it.

'So, Mummy,' she said, brightly, 'your turn next. Where are we going for your clothes?'

'Oh…' her mother waved a hand. 'I thought I might just have a few things made up by Mrs. Farthing.'

'Aren't you going to choose some lovely things from your favourite boutiques in Bond Street?'

'Alice, we've been in that huge shop for four hours. I am not doing any more shopping today.' Her mother smiled and squeezed Alice's hand. 'I'm so glad we found you such pretty clothes; you are so lovely to look at, it would be a waste not to dress you well.'

'You are a darling,' said Alice, kissing her mother's cheek. They sat, hand in hand until they reached the house, where the butler came out to open the car doors for them. He and a young male house servant emptied the taxi of all its packages while Alice and her mother walked through to the sitting room and rang the bell for tea.

Mrs. De Bonneville sat down in her favourite armchair and glanced at the clock. 'Your father should be home soon,' she said. 'He'll want to see what you got.'

'Won't he find ladies' clothes very dull?'

'Not at all: he was expressing his concern earlier in the week, that you would need a whole new wardrobe for your new life.'

'He's very thoughtful, isn't he?'

'He is a very kind man, yes. We do both love you very much, Alice: I hope you know that.'

Alice's mother wasn't known for making personal statements about her feelings. Alice had to fight back tears.

'I'm going to miss you and Daddy so much,' she said simply, getting up from her chair and going over to wrap her arms around her mother. She didn't dare to say anything more, for fear her mother would comprehend the extent of her emotional turmoil. Whilst she felt like she would burst from her longing to be reunited with her beloved Henry, there was a part of her which couldn't bear the thought of being separated from her parents – and by such a distance, and for who knew how long?

Chapter Sixteen

'We love your drawings,' said the editor, sitting across the table. She had Fleur's portfolio open in front of her, and now she pointed to one of Fleur's illustrations, which depicted a swallow in flight, carrying a basket of cookies with its feet. 'Tell me about this one.'

'Oh, that's Matilda Swallow. She delivers baked goods to the whole village.'

'I see. Can you tell me anything else about Matilda?'

'Oh, well, she likes Tchaikovsky but can't stand Beethoven – she thinks him overblown. Also, she wears a funny little headscarf on windy days, but she adores the rain, and loves to get soaked to the skin.'

'You have a wonderful imagination. Do you have any books of your own?' the editor continued. 'Ones you've written as well as illustrated, I mean?'

'No: I've only done illustrations. I don't really see myself as a writer.'

'Well, that shouldn't be a problem. We have a number of excellent writers on our list, so I'm sure we can sort out a collaboration partner for you.'

'Does that mean you're definitely signing me?'

'If you'd like to illustrate for us, then we'd love to have you.' She held out a hand for Fleur to shake.

'That's fantastic,' said Fleur. She shook the proffered hand.

'I have to say, I love your outfit,' said the editor. 'Is it vintage?'

'Pretty much my whole wardrobe belonged to either my mother or my grandmother. They kept all their clothes, so there are pieces dating back to the nineteen-twenties: flapper dresses and cloche hats. Then there are sixties' pieces, like this dress and jacket.'

'You lucky thing.'

'Thank you: I am lucky, aren't I? I have such fun, choosing my outfit each day.'

'I wonder – would you be interested in illustrating a fashion book for us? We have been approached by the V&A with the idea of producing one, and you seem just the person for the job. Have you done any fashion sketches?'

'Only for my own amusement.'

'Do you have anything to show me?'

Fleur leaned across the table and pulled some pieces of sketch paper from a pocket inside her portfolio case. She passed them to the editor, who scanned them at once.

'Oh, these are lovely.'

'Thank you. I've always had a passion for sketching female silhouettes – that nineteen-forties' shape, in particular: with the pinched-in waist and the wide shoulders.'

'It is truly iconic, isn't it? Mind you, the same could be said for your outfit today – Jackie O, nineteen-sixties, if I'm not mistaken? That pillbox-style hat was a particular favourite of hers, wasn't it?'

'That's right.' They smiled at each other. 'I would love to work on a fashion book if you are going ahead with the project,' said Fleur.

'Well, I think that now we have our illustrator, we'd be foolish not to, don't you? I'll get back in touch with the publications officer at the V&A, and get an idea of timeframe, designers to focus on, and so on.' She leaned across the desk to shake Fleur's hand. 'It's been an absolute pleasure; thank you so much for coming in.'

'Thank you for inviting me – I feel quite excited now.'

'Good – that's how we like our talented authors and illustrators to feel.'

'I don't think I've ever been described as "talented" before.'

'With talent like yours, I think you'd better get used to it.'

The editor escorted Fleur back down in the lift to reception, where they took their farewells. Then Fleur, too excited to sit on a bus, walked all the way back to St Pancras in her snakeskin shoes, which were definitely not designed for long walks on hard pavements. She didn't care, though – her head was reeling with images of beautiful books, filled with her illustrations. This, she knew, was what she was born to do. It was the only thing – apart from baking and gardening – that came as naturally to her as breathing.

Back at the house, her mother's friend was making herself a cup of tea when Fleur arrived. She made one for Fleur, too, and the pair of them sat at the old kitchen table, eating vanilla biscuits that Fleur had made the day before, and talking through the day's events. The dogs had thoroughly enjoyed their walk that morning and had been treated to another walk in the afternoon.

'I don't think I've had so much exercise in ages,' said the kind lady. 'If you ever want help with Hattie, I'd be delighted.'

'That's so kind – but I'm moving soon.'

'Is that why the house is looking so sparse?'

'Yes: we've been emptying it, in preparation for handing it over, once the sale is completed.'

'It's been lovely having you here in the village – you remind me a little of your mum.'

'She was so fond of you, Venetia,' said Fleur.

'And I of her.' She reached across to squeeze Fleur's hand. 'She would be so proud, to hear of your success with your art. She was always saying what a talent you had, from when you were quite tiny. Do you remember that picture you drew, of me with Boris and Lucille? Those dogs were quite lifelike, yet you can't have been more than eight.'

'I remember. Do you still have it?'

'Of course. It's framed, on my mantelpiece. You even captured something of their cheeky little personalities.'

'I'm glad you like it. They were sweet little dogs.'

'They were, weren't they? Anyway, tell me more about this publishing house you went to.'

Fleur told Venetia all about the meeting, and about how she looked set to produce fashion plates for a book for the V&A. This last bit sounded fanciful when she said it aloud. 'I mean... if the V&A approves my illustrations, I suppose.'

'If this editor likes your work, I daresay that's a given.'

'I really don't know. As you know, I've only worked on children's picture books, so I've never had a client in that way, just a writer-collaborator and a publisher.'

'Well, I'm sure it will all be fine. Now, I must head off.'

Fleur escorted her to the front door, where Venetia paused to give her a kiss on the cheek, before remarking: 'You do look wonderful in that outfit, Fleur. You have a marvellous way with clothes.'

Chapter Seventeen

RMS Arundel Castle

5 September, 1928

Dear Henry,

Why am I writing to you, when I am on the ship that will bring me to you, and you will never receive the letter? I plan to write to you almost every day, however – perhaps I will make you a present of these missives when finally we are reunited.

You may be interested to learn that we have followed your advice about the ginger root. In fact, one of the ship's crew has shown us how to make a brew, by steeping the root in hot water. This makes it far more palatable. We have shared this wisdom with many of the other passengers. There are those, however, who are already so sick with the motion, they can do nothing but lie in their berths. Meanwhile, your bride and her parents stroll around the decks as if they were seasoned sailors!

My own cabin is far grander than I had imagined. There is even a small bath tub in the room, with hot, running water!

Mummy and Daddy have come across some old friends onboard – the Smyth-Loames – do you know them? My parents keep dashing off to play tennis with them, which just means that I have more time to write to you. Sadly, the Smyth-Loames have a son of around my age, called Rodney. They are very keen for us to spend time together and seem quite to ignore the fact of my engagement to you. I suspect their 'dear Rodney' is a burden to them, and they can't wait to marry him off to some poor, unsuspecting girl. Well, they shall have to find some other sacrificial lamb – this one has already been spoken for.

Mama has acquired a lovely gown to wear for the wedding: she will be quite beautiful. It took me an age to persuade her that she should have something fine for herself – she, who has been so keen to ensure I have only the most flattering wardrobe for my trousseau. I hope you will like my wedding dress… I will say no more, except to tell you that it was not acquired for the occasion, but was a gift from an old friend of Mama's, called Mrs. Larkin. I love it and am especially touched to have been entrusted with such a precious gift.

I am crossing off the days in my journal until I will see you – although the Captain has explained that it does depend on our having the right winds to help us along. Apparently, a strong wind that blows in the wrong direction will slow down our progress – even with such a large ship as the 'Arundel Castle'. I can't wait to see you – and yet wait I must.

I shall write again tomorrow – by which time we shall have dined at the Captain's table. I shall wear one of my best new gowns for the occasion.

I think of you constantly, and try to imagine what you are doing and how your fellow workers look and act. I am jealous of them all, for having your attention, when I want it all to myself but can have none of it! I try to picture our house, with its veranda, and the screens we must put up, against the mosquitoes. Most of all, my darling Henry, I picture your face.

Your loving fiancée,

Alice

My darling Henry,

If I have to spend a moment longer in the obsequious company of Rodney Smyth-Loames, I swear I will scream!

He was seated next to me at last night's dinner at the Captain's table and did nothing to ingratiate himself with me – although he appeared convinced I could not fail to be charmed by his insincere flatteries.

You will be interested to learn that my hair is, 'the gleaming brown of a horse chestnut', my hands 'as pale and lovely as lilies', and my eyes (here he struggled for a moment, to find a suitable comparison) 'the green of dewy grass'. Insufferable man! He knows I am engaged, and that I am travelling purely to be married. Fortunately, the Smyth-Loames disembark before Alexandria, so I will be rid of his unwanted attentions by the time I reach you.

Until then, my love, I remain yours entirely,

Alice

RMS *Arundel Castle*

13 September, 1928

My dearest Henry,

Several days have passed, and I have not written. The truth is, that I had nothing to report! The sea continues in its watery way; the sun continues to shine; the ship continues in its artificial throwing-together of people who would otherwise surely never seek one another's company.

I have read all of the books that I brought along for the voyage and am reduced to sifting through the ship's ill-stocked library, attempting to pick out novels from among the numerous books on engineering and history. Part of me feels I should be reading up on mechanics, in order to appear slightly more knowledgeable among your colleagues. However, I plucked one such book from the shelf and found it so densely filled with charts and numbers, that I gave up after a very short time. You shall have to make do with a wife who is very ignorant about the workings of cars, I'm afraid. I shall, however, endeavour to make up for this want in knowledge with a marked enthusiasm: I shall be the wife who listens to every detail of every bolt (or whatever is used to fix together the parts of cars).

Until there is something of interest to put down on these pages, my love, I shall abstain from writing. However, I remain,

your Alice

RMS Arundel Castle

16 September, 1928

Darling Henry,

Some news at last (albeit not of a merry sort)! Mama has fallen out with Mrs. Smyth-Loames. This was inevitable, I'm afraid. Mrs. S-L possesses one of those formidable personalities, in the face of which one either bows or resists. Mother, I am satisfied to say, has resisted: hence, this impasse. Neither will apologise and as I am quite sure the fault is all on the side of Mrs. S-L, who believes herself always right, I can only assume there is little chance of a détente's being reached in the foreseeable future.

Whilst Papa still slips off to see Mr. S-L (Mama knows of this, but turns a blind eye), Mama and I sit on the deck with our books or seek out entertainment in the ballroom. There is a very good band onboard, and she and I enjoy listening to their large and varied repertoire.

There is nothing more to report; therefore, I will sign off for today.

Yours in love,

Alice

RMS Arundel Castle

20 September, 1928

My darling Henry,

The next port we pull into will be Alexandria!

Oh, Henry, I feel as though a strong magnet is drawing me towards you. You are my magnetic North Pole…

Apart from my new wardrobe, I am very little changed. You, however, after the influences of such a place as Egypt – how might you be changed! Will it take me long, to learn the customs of my new home? I fear I may be an embarrassment to you at first, as I commit faux-pas, in my ignorance of local culture.

You talk of Mr. Mohamed's wife, Fatima, who is to be my guide to Alexandria and the Egyptian mores. It is so very kind of her to offer to take me under her wing. I hope she will not be too disappointed at my lack of knowledge – I shall be a dedicated student, and intend to learn quickly.

I am glad that I shall never post this letter, Henry: you should not be bothered with these trivial concerns of mine when you have so many demands competing for your attention.

Meanwhile, I listen to the band with Mama, or lie in my berth and read novels, or write these letters that will never be posted. They are my journal, my musings on both my future and my present. This, however, is a present of unreality: the ship a temporary life which suspends time. We are travellers between points in our lives, rather than enjoying any true existence while onboard.

Enough of these philosophical ramblings!

It only remains to say that I love you, Henry Pemberton and that I can hardly wait to become Mrs. Henry Pemberton.

All my love forever,

Alice

***

1928

As she descended the gangplank in Alexandria, Alice was assailed by the sounds and scents of the port. A large market was in full swing close by, no doubt hoping to attract the custom of the tourists from the cruise ships. She could smell spices and fruits, and strong perfumes, all mingling in the shimmering heat. She and her parents were surrounded almost immediately by turbaned men in long, white tunics, who called to them in Egyptian accents, offering to sell them:

'Beautiful carvings, look!' or 'Gold necklaces, very cheap!'

The ship's porters, who were wheeling the luggage in huge, laden trolleys, shouted to the pedlars in an Arabic that, even to Alice's untrained ears, sounded very English in intonation.

It took her a moment to spot Henry. He stood apart – a space around him as if even the market traders were a little awed by this distinguished presence among them. Alice felt a jolt of love and pride, as she saw how handsome, how broad-shouldered Henry was, in his lightweight cream Panama hat and a pale linen suit. He provided a cool contrast to the bright colours of the goods on the market stalls, like a drink of iced water on a hot day. And it was such a hot day: the sun scorching so that Alice's own wide-brimmed hat and dainty parasol did little to protect her from its rays.

Henry shouldered his way through the crowds to meet them, greeting first Alice's parents and then throwing his arms around her. She felt his arms, strong around her, and his chest beneath her cheek, and wanted to hold on to him, to breathe in his scent of Brilliantine and shaving cream. He leaned down and kissed her briefly, on the lips, but then he let her go and addressed her parents:

'Come on, this way,' he said, 'I have some cabs waiting.' He led the way to a row of long, black cars, into which he instructed the porters to load the baggage. He helped Mrs. De Bonneville into the front passenger seat of the car at the head of the line, and Alice into the back, where he and Thomas joined her. He sat in the middle, and Alice relished the sensation of his arm and leg, pressed up against hers. He placed his hand around her gloved one, and she closed her eyes in pleasure to feel that he was really here, beside her.

'I've booked you into the Hotel San Stefano,' he told them, as they drove. 'It's the best hotel in Alexandria, and has a lovely view of the sea.'

'That sounds lovely,' said Alice's mother. 'I can't believe we've finally made it. I still feel as if we're on the boat – that rocking feeling.'

'That will take a while to wear off,' said Henry. 'Especially after such a long crossing.'

'And the heat,' said her mother. 'Is it always this hot?'

'Sometimes it's hotter,' said Henry. 'There are fans in the hotel, which should help. If you look out now, you will see that most of the buildings are constructed in white stone, to deflect the worst of the heat.'

The drive was a stop-start affair, hampered by unwary pedestrians and even chickens and goats, wandering about the road. Henry kept Alice's hand folded inside his own, like a secret. Now and then, he turned to her, and they gazed into one another's eyes, and she felt her world shrink as if there was no one else in the world but the two of them.

At last, they drew up in front of a large, white, ornate building, decorated with columns and balconies.

'Here we are,' said Henry, 'the San Stefano.' The hotel faced the Eastern Harbour along a promenade which Henry told them was known as the Corniche. As Alice climbed out into the blazing sunshine, she marvelled at the blue of the sea and sky, contrasting with the paleness of the sand and the buildings.

'Is everything here either blue or white?' she asked Henry.

He laughed. 'There does tend to be little change in the sky, from what I've seen so far. I've heard it's a bit different in the rainy season, mind you. That's meant to be next month, so I'd enjoy the blue September skies while we have them.'

Hotel porters came out in droves, to take in the luggage from the cabs. Meanwhile, Henry escorted Alice and her parents into the hotel.

'I hope you'll be all right here,' he said. 'I asked around, and was told this was the best place.'

'I'm sure we'll be fine,' said Thomas. 'It looks clean and well-presented.'

They were greeted by friendly hotel staff, who spoke fluent English, and made them feel like honoured guests. Henry took his farewell, promising to return in time for dinner.

They were escorted up to the third floor, where the lift doors opened on to splendid views of the harbour, through large picture windows.

'What a beautiful place,' commented Alice's father, as the hotel porters unlocked the door to their room.

'We're just next door if you need anything,' Alice's mother told her, and she and Thomas vanished into their suite.

Soon, Alice found herself alone in her room, throwing open the doors to her own private balcony.

'I'm here!' she told herself. 'I'm finally here!'

Chapter Eighteen

Dougie was scrabbling at the floor beside the front door before Fleur had even heard Toby's Land Rover approaching. By the time the car had pulled into the turning circle in front of the house, the dog was whining quietly – too well-bred to let out the howl he no doubt longed to emit.

Fleur judged it safest to wait until Toby had turned off the car engine before opening the front door. The moment she let Dougie out, he raced a blur of grey the size of a small pony, to intercept his owner.

Toby stepped down from the Land Rover and crouched to greet Dougie, who was so well-trained that he didn't even jump up at his owner. Toby stroked the dog's head and ears.

'Hey, boy, did you miss me? I missed you, too.' He glanced up at Fleur, who had stepped outside after Dougie, and was watching this affectionate reunion. Today, she was dressed in a wide-leg orange floral jumpsuit from Biba. She'd also found a pair of knee-length leather boots, made by Jones Bootmaker. She'd done her hair in a long plait, which trailed over her right shoulder. A large, floppy hat and a pair of hoop earrings completed the nineteen-seventies' look.

'Looking cool,' said Toby, smiling at her. 'Very Bohemian. Your grandmother's outfit?'

'No, these were Mum's clothes. Aren't they great? I feel like a member of *Charlie's Angels*. I'm just waiting for my orders from Charlie.'

'Well, you certainly look glamorous enough. I don't remember the stars of the TV series being famed for their fighting or investigating skills…'

'A good job, too. I can bake a decent cake, though. Why don't you come in for a cup of tea, and you can try the carrot cake I made this morning?' She pointed at Hattie, who was barking loudly, and running excitably around the assembled figures. 'I'm also not sure Hattie's ready to say goodbye just yet.'

Toby checked his watch. 'I'd love to…'

'…but you've got somewhere to be,' Fleur finished for him.

Toby straightened up from petting his wolfhound.

'I'm sorry – especially after you've done me such a huge favour, by having Dougie. But there's a Skype meeting I have to be home for – it's with a big client.'

'Anyone I've heard of?'

'Sir Terence Conran. He's planning to open a new restaurant, in Manchester, and it looks like I've won the pitch.'

'That's amazing.'

'Thank you. I'm holding my breath until the paperwork's signed, but it does all look positive so far.'

'What sort of designs have you come up with for him?'

'Why don't you come over later, and I'll show you if you like? I can cook dinner. Bring Hattie, and she and Dougie can eat together.'

184

Fleur hesitated. 'I was meant to be going to my Zumba class.'

'I didn't know you did Zumba.'

'It's only my second class.'

He held up his hands, to show there were no hard feelings. 'Another time, then.'

'Thank you: that would be good.'

Toby walked over to the connecting gate to his own garden, which he opened to let Dougie through. Then he walked back to his Land Rover and turned his vehicle carefully around the turning circle before heading back along the drive.

Hattie ran over to the connecting gate, which Toby had shut after Dougie. She began hurling herself at the little wooden gate until Fleur was afraid she might hurt herself and ran over to stop her. She pulled at Hattie's collar until the Labrador calmed down.

Hey, girl – you can visit Dougie another time, all right?'

Hattie gave Fleur a baleful look, before lying down on the path in front of the gate and beginning to whine.

'Maybe I should have said yes to that invitation,' Fleur said. 'You'd have been happier, for a start.' She didn't really know what had caused her to say no; she didn't really care about missing her Zumba class. Perhaps it was the fact that Toby seemed rarely to be free – and yet, he expected her to be available at the drop of a nineteen-seventies' floppy-brim hat.

'Come on, Hattie – I have work to do. Are you going to come in with me?' Hattie looked up at her but didn't move. 'All right, girl – I'll see you later.'

Inside, Fleur made a mug of tea in the kitchen, which smelled deliciously of the baking she'd done earlier. She cut herself a piece of the carrot cake, and then, plate in one hand and mug in the other, she headed upstairs to the room at the front of the house, where she had set up her studio. This had been her mother's bedroom. It was a white room, spacious now the furniture had largely been removed, which gave views on to the garden and farm fields beyond, through pretty casement windows.

She walked over to her easel. She was working on her first sketches for the Bloomsbury children's book. The publishing company had efficiently matched her with one of the writers on their list – an expatriate American called Warren Spindler, who wrote wonderfully imaginative, rhyming stories. His first series of books had been all about a little girl called Loretta, who had a magic vegetable patch. Each vegetable conferred its own special power – to make anyone who ate it shrink, for instance or become super-strong or develop the ability to fly.

They had gelled immediately at their first meeting and had experienced barely a pause in their conversation. They had shared reminiscences: their favourite picture books, their most-read children's books, their favourite artists and illustrators and writers.

I'm really excited to work with you, Warren had emailed, after the meeting. *I think we're going to come up with something really special together.* She could hear his American accent in these words. His warm, friendly voice lifted off the page towards her.

Fleur had printed off this email and pinned it to her noticeboard, to remind her she was not working alone. Being an artist could be a lonely business. She loved the creative process – and enjoyed her own company – but sometimes it could be good to have someone on-hand to bounce ideas off, and to swap feedback and encouragement.

The plan was for them to come up with a synopsis and some sketches, to give the Bloomsbury editor an idea of the finished product. Ideally, they would have more than one project to showcase, though Fleur wasn't yet sure how realistic this was. So far, they had the idea for a world of butterflies, in which a pair of children would find a lost caterpillar and take it home. When it hatched – into a giant moth – the children would harness it, and ride it to the rainforest, to find its family.

'*Dr. Dolittle* meets Gerald Durrell,' said Warren. 'A combination of fantasy and a serious, ecological message. I think it will be charming. Your illustrative style will be perfect for this.'

The phone rang and broke her reverie. She picked up the phone to hear her agent's voice on the other end. Her agent was always short of time, and she didn't believe in the usual conventions of a telephone conversation. This time, she began with:

'What's all this about a book for the V&A?'

'Oh, sorry – I should have told you. Bloomsbury might be publishing a book on fashion for the Museum. The editor suggested I might be the person to illustrate it.'

'Well, you need to be aware that all these "mights" have become "wills".'

'Do you mean it's happening?'

'It's happening pronto – the editor wants to meet with you and the V&A publications officer and one of the curators.'

'But that's fantastic!'

'A bit of a remove from kids' picture books, isn't it?'

'Oh…but you will still represent me? For the V&A project, I mean.'

'It's not really my area of expertise, Fleur. You might be better to seek a separate agent for your fashion drawings if you are planning to expand on that side of your work.'

Fleur felt panic set in. In desperation, she begged,

'Please, please, Ruth – I really don't want to have to start finding another agent I like. You were the fourth one I'd tried, remember? The others were so…businessy.'

'I'm not sure how to take that.'

'I just mean that you care about the client, and understand the client's work. The others seemed more concerned with the money.'

'Perhaps if I were more concerned with the money, I might have a full-time assistant by now.'

'If you do this deal for me, you can branch out a bit from picture books, and maybe you'll be able to afford a full-time assistant.'

Her agent laughed. 'OK, I'll do my best – just remember, it's not my…'

'…area of expertise – I've got it. I'm sure you can get me a good deal nonetheless.'

'Let me go and talk to the editor again, and tell her I'll be handling the deal on your behalf. Meanwhile, put next Wednesday at noon in your diary.'

'Is that for the V&A meeting? Are we meeting at the Museum itself?'

'Indeed we are. I think they want to show you the clothes you'll be illustrating.'

'It's a dream project. I don't know how I'll fit it around the work with Warren, though.' Fleur thought about the butterflies picture book and the amount of work involved. She'd been planning on dedicating herself to that project.

'You'll manage. A bit of burning the midnight oil, perhaps, but you'll get there. It sounds as though the two of you really hit it off – the editor at Bloomsbury told me he was enthusing about you.'

Fleur felt her cheeks burn. 'Really? He is very nice.'

'Is there a pairing in the air?'

'If you mean a purely professional pairing, based on mutual respect for one another's work, then definitely,' said Fleur primly.

'You don't give much away, do you?'

'Not if I can help it. Now, don't you have some other poor illustrator to harass?'

'I'm going, I'm going… Remember: V&A, twelve noon, next Wednesday.'

'I'll remember.'

***

Fleur had barely seen Toby since he'd picked up Dougie the week before. Occasionally, they waved to one another as he pulled in or out of his driveway while she was out walking Hattie.

On the other hand, the phone calls and emails from her book collaborator, Warren, had been prolific. He was astonishingly creative, and ideas seemed to spill out of him like honey from an upturned jar.

'I was thinking the girl in the butterflies book might be blind,' he said in one call. 'She finds the butterfly world by the scent of the flowers that grow there.'

'I like that.'

'I wonder if Bloomsbury could stretch the production budget, to add texture to the pages – that would be important to Adwoa.'

'Adwoa?'

'Oh, that's her name – if you like it, too. And I thought the boy could be called Nelson.'

'You have it all planned out.'

'Sorry – I just get a bit overexcited. Feel free to rein me in.'

'No, it's great to hear your enthusiasm. Let's go with all of it for now. I've done some mock-ups of how I see the butterfly forest – I'll scan them and email them over to you.'

Fleur had dreamt the butterfly world before drawing it – it had invaded her dreams, in shades of pink, purple and silver, with glitter like fairy dust on the butterflies' wings. Rough though these first drawings were, they were also some of the best illustrations she'd ever done. She felt inspired and excited, and, since those first dreams of the butterfly world, she had been finding it hard to sleep: her brain kept up a restless film reel of butterflies blooming like flora on trees, and hordes of caterpillars shredding leaves; of two children in their pyjamas climbing aboard a giant moth; of a constantly moving rainbow made up of thousands of winged insects.

When she wasn't dreaming butterflies and caterpillars, she was online, investigating the collections of the Victoria & Albert Museum and sketching the clothes she found there. From the nineteenth-century bustles and bonnets to the twentieth century's ever-evolving styles, the V&A had it all. She didn't yet know what the focus of the book was to be, but she was keen to familiarise herself with at least a small proportion of the collection before her meeting with the Museum's publications officer and curator.

When the day of the meeting came, she donned a full-skirted, below-knee-length dress in a vibrant orange with large white polka dots. She teamed the dress with white gloves, white T-bar shoes and a neat white box-shape handbag. A little orange shrug-style cardigan, a white bangle and white Bakelite earrings completed the nineteen-fifties' look.

When she arrived, and despite all her research, nothing had prepared Fleur for the sheer scale of the V&A's fashion collection. The curator led her from display to display, talking her through minute changes in the length or shape of a sleeve, or the way a décolletage could be either de rigueur or taboo, depending on the era or location in which you lived.

They explored room after room of dresses, from the extensive, beautifully crafted wardrobe of early-twentieth-century London socialite, Heather Firbank, to the designs of Mary Quant and Biba Hulanicki in the nineteen-sixties and -seventies. There were wedding dresses by Vera Wang and Vivienne Westwood, and iconic Chanel skirt suits.

Then the curator led Fleur to the accessories rooms. Here, Fleur stopped in front of one of the hat displays – a collection of toques, cloches and pillbox hats – that was especially appealing. The hats were delicate and pretty – lightweight fabric had been combined with elegant ornaments, to striking effect. She read the label on the case: *Debonair Designs*.

'That was my family's hat business!' she exclaimed.

The curator walked over to join her. 'Really, your family ran Debonair Designs?' he asked.

'Yes! It was my great-grandparents' business. I can't believe they're here.'

'Well, Debonair was an important millinery business, especially in the nineteen-twenties and 'thirties. They developed two lines – one for the more mature, traditional woman, and the other for the fashionable younger woman, who wanted to push the boundaries a bit.'

'Like my grandmother,' said Fleur. 'I wonder if she had any input into the business.'

'I might be able to find out if you like? There might be something in the archives.'

'That would be wonderful – yes, please. She used to talk about her parents' hat business, but I don't remember her mentioning playing any part herself. I have her letters, and I think in one of them, she did say her mother was considering letting her do some designing. My grandmother Alice was a very fashion-conscious woman, so it's hard to imagine her not having strong opinions on whatever her parents were producing.'

'I'll see what I can dig out.'

'Thank you.'

After the grand tour, the curator led her to a meeting room, where Fleur's agent was sitting with a woman whom Fleur rightly presumed to be the publications officer. They shook hands, and then shared a platter of sandwiches while the publications lady detailed the plans for the forthcoming book. Now and then, the curator chipped in, with additional detail.

'So it's a fashion-through-the-ages book,' said the publications officer. 'With beautiful photographs from our collection.'

'What will make this book stand out from all the other books on fashion history?' asked Fleur's agent. You mean, apart from the fact that we're the V&A?' asked the publications woman. 'Don't forget, we boast the largest and most comprehensive collection in the world. I believe that any publication bearing our name is guaranteed to be desirable. The Museum is associated with quality and knowledge – we always ensure any publication bearing the V&A stamp is of the highest standard, written and vetted by our in-house experts.'

'Of course,' said the agent, sounding slightly flustered. Fleur was interested to see her agent out of her depth: after all, this was a woman who had taken on some of the biggest figures in the publishing industry and cut some excellent deals for her clients.

The curator shook his head. 'No, you're quite right – we do have to ensure the book stands out. The market is flooded with books on the history of fashion. Where we hope to differ, is in the sheer breadth of subject matter we plan to cover. This is not some slim coffee-table publication, but a large volume, intended as reference material for fashion lecturers and students the world over.'

'I see,' said Fleur's agent. 'So it's a big project… Where does Fleur come in?'

'Well,' said the publications officer, 'We'd like the cover to feature a collage-effect of fashion sketches. We could use the obvious ones – Oscar de la Renta, Miu Miu, and so on. However, we thought it would work well to have our own sketches – ones that no one has seen before.'

'So, is it just the cover?' Fleur asked.

'No, not at all: that's just the beginning. We're going to have a fashion plate at the start of every chapter – and there will be a lot of chapters. We haven't decided yet, but we may also want some sketches scattered throughout the body of the chapters.'

The negotiations started, and the curator excused himself, leaving the others to sort out the finances. Fleur sat in silence. The figures that were being bandied around sounded preposterous – surely no one was proposing to pay her so many thousands of pounds, for this hugely enjoyable project?

She started to daydream about sketching some of the staff who worked at the Museum – she'd seen some interesting faces when they were looking around. Out of the blue, she found herself addressed by her agent:

'Are you happy with that, Fleur?'

'With what? Sorry – I was miles away.'

Her agent named an even more astronomical sum than had earlier been mentioned, and Fleur endeavoured to appear complacent – as if she received vast sums of money as a regular occurrence.

'Yes, that sounds fine,' she said, airily.

'And we'll pay expenses, too, of course,' said the publications officer.

'Great,' said Fleur. 'Thank you.'

The meeting ended, and Fleur wandered out of the room, leaving her agent taking a long time over her goodbyes. For a woman with little knowledge of fashion publishing, she certainly knew how to drive a hard bargain.

Her eye attracted by a nearby display of beautiful silk saris, Fleur pulled out her sketchbook and began to draw. She was so engrossed, that the curator had to call her name twice before she registered.

'Ms. Cavendish? Fleur?' he said.

'Oh, hello again.'

'Hello. I found this, and I thought you might be interested. It is a list of staff employed at Debonair from 1925 to '30. This is a photocopy, so you can keep it.'

'Thank you, that's great.' Fleur smiled at him and took the list of names. After he'd walked away, she started to scan the names. One listing caught her eye: *Alice De Bonneville, Chief Designer, Debonair Debutantes' Collection.*

So, her grandmother had worked for the family business. Perhaps some of the hats Fleur had inherited were her grandmother's own design. This was a heartening thought, as she stepped out into the September rain and bid farewell to her agent before setting off for the station and her journey home to Wisteria Cottage.

Chapter Nineteen

1928

'What do you think?' Henry gazed down anxiously at Alice. They were standing outside the church, in which they were to be married in two days' time.

'It looks very sweet. Can we go in?' she asked.

'Of course.' He led her to the porch of the little church and opened the wooden door. They stepped into the interior, which smelt of candles and polish. It was dark and cool, and Alice relished the contrast with the stifling air outside.

She took it all in: the wooden pews, the statue of the Virgin Mary at the front, and the painstakingly embroidered cushions. There was one stained-glass window at the front, above the altar, and its colours painted themselves across the flagstone floor, like watercolours. The ceiling was domed and beautifully painted, and there were white marble columns.

'It's perfect,' she said, smiling up at her fiancé.

The worried crease in his brow faded and he smiled down at her. 'I was so worried you wouldn't like it. It's rather small.'

'That's why it's perfect. I'm marrying you – I don't need a huge cathedral, to help me appreciate how lucky I am, and how special our wedding day will be.'

'I love you, Alice De Bonneville.'

'And I love you, too, Henry Pemberton.' She gazed up at him and saw a shadow creep behind the happiness on his face. 'Are you sad that your parents can't be here?' she asked.

'A little. But Father has been frail for so long, I knew it wouldn't be wise for them to attempt the journey.'

'Shall we light a candle for him now?'

They walked over to the candles, which were slightly yellow, and varied in size, depending on how many times they had been used. Henry chose the tallest, least-used one. He struck a match and closed his eyes, and Alice placed a hand on his shoulder and closed her own eyes, as they both prayed silently for his father's health and his parents' happiness. Her own happiness, she felt sure, was something she didn't need to pray for: not with Henry by her side.

Afterwards, they met up with her parents, and they all strolled along the Corniche, admiring the evening sun's sparkle on the clear water.

That night, before dinner, Alice's mother came to her hotel room. She sat on Alice's bed and looked up at her.

'How do you feel about everything, darling?'

'I can't believe how lucky I am – to be marrying such a kind, wonderful man.'

Her mother smiled. 'He is a very kind man. I'm sure you will be happy together. But will you be all right here, in Alexandria? Don't forget, Henry will be at work most days. What will you do with yourself?'

Alice sat down beside her mother on the bed and took her hand. 'I think I'll be fine. It's bound to be a bit lonely at first, but Henry says the wives of his management team are all looking forward to meeting me. One of them is Egyptian, so I can learn about the culture while I'm here. It's all so new to me… And then there's the house to sort out.'

'When will we see the house?'

'I'm not sure we will see it, before the wedding! Henry says the workmen have promised to move out tomorrow, but apparently they're not very reliable. The good news is that it's not far out – I'll be able to walk into town, on cooler days.'

'Is it all right, to walk alone here? I'm not sure if that's safe.'

'Mummy, stop worrying about me. I won't do anything without checking first with the other wives.'

'Do you promise?'

Alice leaned over to kiss her mother's cheek.

'I promise.'

'I'm going to miss you,' said her mother, quietly.

'I know. I'll miss you, too. But let's not think about that, now. I want the next few days to be happy ones.'

Her mother put on her best faux-mournful expression:

'All right, darling – I shall wear my best smile in two days' time when I marry off my only daughter and have only another week before I leave her behind in a foreign country!'

'Stop it, Mummy!'

Her mother smiled. 'It's lovely to see you so happy. I shall remind myself of that, whenever I start to miss you, once I'm back home.'

'And you could come out again – maybe next year?'

'Perhaps. I'll talk to your father about it. Anyway, hadn't we better change for dinner? It's gone seven o'clock.'

She left to get changed. Alice slipped off her day dress and drew one of her new gowns from her wardrobe. She slid the cool cloth over her head, fastened the little buttons at the back, and stood before the full-length mirror. The dress was in a delicate rose-pink, decorated with an intricate pattern of tiny, hand-stitched silver beads. Even her mother had agreed that this dress was a work of art when they'd spotted it in the window of a tiny boutique in South Kensington, whilst shopping for bags. The pink suited her complexion perfectly. She sat at the dressing table and applied a pink lipstick, to tone with her dress, plus a little rouge to give more colour to her pale, English-rose cheeks. Then she combed out her neat bob and stood up. Her parents knocked at her door, and she called to them to come in.

'I just have to put on my shoes and hat. I have gloves somewhere... She rummaged in a drawer in the wardrobe and found a pair of pale-pink silk gloves. Silver sandals and a pink cloche and shawl completed the look.

'You look beautiful,' her father said, kissing her cheek. 'Just like your mother.'

It was true: her mother did look lovely. She was dressed in a midnight-blue lace dress, with a defined waist. She had accessorised with a pearl necklace and matching earrings.

'I am proud of my ladies,' said Mr. De Bonneville, with his wife on one arm and his daughter on the other, as they walked along the corridor to the lift that would take them up to the restaurant on the top floor of the hotel.

The views as the lift doors opened were even more spectacular than on their own floor of the hotel. Floor-to-ceiling windows revealed an expanse of sea that sparkled, wide and blue, before them.

'It feels like I could just step out on to the sea – like on to a beautiful blue carpet,' said Alice.

'I know what you mean,' agreed her father. 'I've never seen a view like it.'

'It is quite magical,' said her mother.

They were shown to a table by the window, where Henry awaited them. He stood up as they approached, and greeted them all. His gaze hovered for a long time on his bride-to-be.

'You look beautiful,' he whispered, from behind his menu, when they were all choosing their dishes.

'Thank you. You look very dashing yourself.' In his bow tie and tuxedo, he was especially handsome. She felt like the luckiest woman alive.

Chapter Twenty

It was a fine September afternoon: like Midas, the sun turned all that it touched to gold. Toby had come by the house, to invite Fleur and Hattie to accompany him and Dougie on a walk. Now, Fleur and Toby were strolling through the woodland on the outskirts of the village, having let the dogs off the lead. Hattie and Dougie were having a wonderful time, barking at squirrels and chasing birds. The woodland was cool, and smelled of wild honeysuckle and earth.

'I want your opinion on something,' said Toby to Fleur. He sat on a fallen tree trunk and gestured for her to join him. He was looking very fine, in a dark-blue shirt and beige chinos.

'What is it?' she asked, as she took her perch beside him. She was wearing a red-and-white stripe polo-neck beneath a sleeveless black mini-dress. On her legs, she wore red tights beneath patent, black, over-the-knee boots. She stretched out her legs to admire the effect.

'You know this restaurant I'm designing in Manchester?' he began.

She relaxed her legs to give him her full attention. 'I do.'

'Well, do you think I should rent a place there for a while, just until the project is underway and I'm happy with the progress?'

She met his gaze in surprise. 'Why are you asking me?'

He looked down at his feet. 'I just thought you might have an opinion on the matter.'

'Hattie will miss Dougie if you do go away for a while.'

'Will she?'

'And I will miss Dougie's owner,' she said quietly.

He raised his eyes to hers and, in his expression, she saw hope mingle with relief.

'I really do like spending time with you,' she told him, her chest tight with all that she wanted to tell him, but felt too shy to say. She had developed feelings for this handsome, kind, talented man – and it was only now that she admitted to herself how strong those feelings were.

'And I like spending time with you,' he told her. He paused, clearly searching for the right words. At last, he said, 'It's more than that.'

She felt her own hope rise. 'What about Marissa?' she asked him.

'Marissa?' He pushed a strand of dark hair back from his forehead, looking confused.

'Your friend from the housewarming. She is keen on you, isn't she?'

'Is she?'

She laughed. 'Did you really not notice?'

He shook his head. 'No…' He thought for a moment. 'I mean, she always invades my space, but I thought that was just how she is...'

'I don't think it's just that – I think she wants to *be* in your space. With you, I mean.'

'Oh… I didn't realise…'

'Does that make a difference? Do you like her?'

'Only as a friend – she's a bit high-maintenance… She likes to provoke a reaction, and often seems to be falling out with one friend or other.'

'I see.'

'Also, she's the ex of one of my mates, so I've never seen her like that – as a romantic possibility, I mean.'

'Poor Marissa.'

'What about you? Do you see me like that?' he asked her.

She gazed into his lovely, dark eyes. 'I do,' she said quietly. He leaned over to kiss her, but Hattie leapt up between them, forcing them apart.

Fleur laughed. 'I think Marissa must have been training Hattie to keep us apart.'

'Either that or Hattie's jealous.'

'What? You think she wants to kiss you herself?' joked Fleur.

'I don't think she wants anyone to kiss *you*,' Toby corrected her. 'You're her human, and no one else's.'

'She might have to get over that notion,' said Fleur, pushing Hattie down and pulling Toby towards her. Their arms went around each other, and they kissed, at last, ignoring Hattie's excited barks. Eventually, Dougie came over and persuaded the Labrador to leave the humans alone. The dogs vanished off to race one another among the trees and sprawling rhododendrons.

Fleur's lips tingled with the excitement of Toby's kiss. She wanted the sensation to go on for hours. Too soon, however, Toby broke away.

'Much as I'd like to stay here forever,' he said softly, 'it's getting dark and we'd better head back.'

They stood up and called to the dogs, clipping on their leads and heading home. All the way, Toby kept his arm around her shoulders, and she could feel his delicious warmth: a layer of protection against the cool evening air.

As they walked, she said,

'You know, you shouldn't make your decisions around me.'

'Why not?'

'Well, there's no point in arranging to be here as much as possible, when I'm about to move away.'

'Really?' He stopped and looked down at her. 'Is it as soon as that?'

'It's next week.'

'Where will you go?' he asked.

'I'm going to pay long visits to each of my siblings, and then make a decision about where I want to settle on a long-term basis.'

'We'll still see each other,' he said. 'Wherever you are, I will come to see you – if that's all right.'

'That's very all right,' she said, smiling up at him. He bent to draw her close and kissed her again. Hattie began to bark, and they broke away, grinning.

'Well, I'd better get on with making the arrangements for the restaurant,' he said. He kissed her quickly before taking his leave with Dougie. Fleur was smiling and distracted as she went inside, made a mug of tea, and headed upstairs to the studio with Hattie at her heels.

The butterfly book was coming on well – even better than she'd imagined – and the effect of each spread of drawings was like a beautiful jigsaw, all the pieces fitting together perfectly to form intricate images and patterns. Tiny caterpillars hid among foliage while pupae hung from trees and translucent butterflies spread their wings. In the midst of this magical scene, the children, tiny and brave, stood out as mini-adventurers. Warren, the writer, had loved her early roughs:

Oh wow, wow, wow, he'd emailed, *these are A-MAZING! I love, love, love them. Please carry on just like this. I can feel the words coming even faster, now I've seen these. The writing is rhyming at the moment, but that can be changed if it's not required. Still, it's fantastic to put scenery to the language... KEEP UP THE GOOD WORK!!*

She had printed off this email, too, and pinned it to her noticeboard beside the other one from Warren. Publishing, she had learnt, was a world of rejection – if you received any positive feedback, it was important to celebrate it and revisit it whenever possible.

There was a ring on the doorbell and she ran downstairs, just behind Hattie, who was barking wildly. It didn't take a genius to guess that Hattie's beloved Dougie must be on the doorstep, presumably with Toby.

As soon as Fleur opened the door, Hattie shot out and ran around excitedly with Dougie. Meanwhile, Toby looked at Fleur and said,

'I'd been meaning to ask if you'd like to go for a drive with me tomorrow.'

'In what? Oooh – in your Jaguar?'

'Actually, I was wondering if you'd like to go out in a much older car: if you'd like to take your Chevy.'

Fleur hesitated. There had seemed something private in her thoughts of driving Miss Chevrolet. Then she saw Toby's face – how anxious he seemed to make her happy – and she relented. 'That would be lovely. I have to warn you, though – I'm not sure she'll drive.'

'Leave that to me.'

'Do you know something about old Chevies?'

'I maintain the Jaguar myself, so I can figure out most problems these old models are likely to suffer from. I'll give the old girl the once-over tonight, once I've sorted out the arrangements for the Manchester job. Is that ok with you?'

'That would be great.'

Chapter Twenty-One

1928

As they left the church after an intimate wedding ceremony, Alice felt as though she might float off into the blue sky, buoyed up with joy. Through a mist of confetti, she caught sight of a magnificent car. It was cream and gleamed in the sunlight. It had a black collapsible top, and a pink ribbon tied in a bow across its long, straight bonnet.

Henry stopped short. 'I don't believe it.'

'Is that for us?' she asked him.

'I think it must be…' With their arms still linked, they walked over to the car, taking in the plush green leather of the seats, and the walnut trim of the dashboard. Henry stopped beside the driver's door and let out a low whistle. 'Isn't she a beauty?' There was an envelope lying on the driver's seat, and he reached in, took hold of the envelope and drew out a card, which he scanned and passed to her. She read it swiftly:

To Mr. and Mrs. Henry Pemberton,
In celebration of your marriage,
and in recognition of Henry's hard
work for General Motors.

Wishing the two of you a long
and prosperous life together,
Yours,
Sebastian Lockswood
and the team at GM

'Is it a Chevrolet?' she asked Henry.

'Indeed it is.' He smiled at her. 'A Chevrolet AB Tourer, if I'm not mistaken. The firm must have had it imported especially. I'm impressed you know your cars. Is there no end to the wonders of you, Alice Pemberton?' He squeezed her arm as he spoke her new name aloud.

She smiled up at him. 'Well, I have been trying to acquire some knowledge of the latest models, now that my new husband is in the trade. There was a model like this in the newspapers recently.'

'So, no doubt you know that this isn't just a Chevrolet, but a very fine one, at that. I wasn't expecting anything like this.'

'They must value you very highly,' said Alice, feeling a rush of pride at being married to this clever, successful man.

'Shall we?' he asked, gesturing to the car.

'I'd love to.'

He opened the passenger door and she climbed in, waiting while he patiently tucked in the excess fabric of her dress. Then he turned the starter handle and climbed into the driver's seat, and they waved to their guests as they drove away. Alice wound down her window,

'See you at The Grand Hotel!' she called to her parents and the other guests who were standing waving. Her veil was tugging hard on her head, as if about to fly off, so she quickly closed her window.

She turned to Henry, 'Will the guests find the hotel all right?'

'It's right on the front – they can't miss it,' he reassured her. He patted the steering wheel. 'Now, what do you think of this for a wedding present?'

'I love it! I seem just to get luckier and luckier. It would have been enough to marry you, without all the wonderful people and presents…'

He shot her a quick smile. 'You are a fine, fine woman, Mrs. Pemberton.'

'Mrs. Pemberton,' she repeated, slowly. 'That's me, now.'

'It certainly is.'

Without warning, he slowed the car and turned into a side road.

'Why are you turning off?' she asked. 'This isn't the way to the front.'

'Don't worry: this won't take long. There's something I want you to see.'

He drove to the end of the road, and then down a little dirt track. At the end, was a white wooden house, with a veranda and a swing seat. Bougainvillea in full bloom clambered over the veranda roof, and jewel-coloured plants in terracotta pots were everywhere. From the high vantage point of the villa, views spread out below.

'Oh!' She cried.

'Do you like it?'

Forgetting all about their guests, Alice said, 'Can I take a look around?'

He checked his watch. 'I think we'd better get back.' He saw the pleading expression on her face and relented. 'All right, then – but quickly, or our guests will think we've abandoned them.'

He walked after her, enjoying the vision of Alice in her wedding dress, running towards the villa, with her veil streaming behind her.

When she reached the house, she turned to wait for the key. He caught her up and unlocked the door, then scooped her up in one, fluid movement, and carried her over the threshold. He was tempted to carry her all the way to the bedroom, but he restrained himself: he wanted to savour their first time in bed together.

'She ran from room to room, exclaiming over the shutters, the furniture – even the mosquito nets.

'It's all so exotic!' she declared at last, as she stood, admiring the view from the bedroom window, which ended at the clear sea and blue sky.

As if suddenly realising that she was in the bedroom with her new husband, Alice stepped back from the window and said,

'We must get to The Grand.'

Henry put his arms around her and held her close, relishing the softness of her against his chest. He leaned down and placed a brief, chaste kiss on her smooth lips. Then, with a sigh, he released her.

'You are quite right, my darling. We'd better go.'

Hand in hand, they walked back to the car, and he drove them over to their assembled wedding party, gathered in a suite at The Grand Hotel.

Alice's mother was waiting in the foyer. 'Thank goodness you're here – I was starting to worry. Where have you been?'

'Henry took me to see our house.'

Her mother's expression changed to one of excitement and curiosity. 'Well? What is it like?'

'It's absolutely perfect!' declared Alice.

Her mother hugged her. 'I'm so glad, darling. Now, shall we greet these guests?'

Arm in arm, they walked into the large room, where guests were milling, glasses of pale liquid in hand. Alcohol was not approved of in Egypt, and so, in place of Champagne, Alice's father had imported a sparkling grape juice produced by a French vineyard.

Alice helped herself to a glass from a tray that was proffered by one of the many waiters. Then she spotted Henry talking to a man and woman. She walked over and was introduced.

'Alice, this is Adam Frederickson – you remember my mentioning Freddie in my letters? He's my right-hand man. And this is his wife, Harriet.' Somebody called Henry's name, and he walked off.

Alice smiled at Freddie as he shook her hand and bowed. He was a small, stocky man, with a large, drooping moustache which gave him a slightly comical appearance. His wife seemed to Alice to embody the opposite of him: she was a tall, fair lady, with a long thin face and a sad expression. Fortunately, Freddie seemed to possess enough joviality for both of them.

'The parts sales enterprise is going splendidly,' he confided to Alice. 'Your husband is a marvel. I have to admit to having been a little anxious, at the prospect of Mr. Locksworth's bringing in a relative unknown. However, Mr. Pemberton has more than proved himself. He is quick to see where costs can be cut, and where the distribution side can be improved upon.'

'I suppose that comes from his experience of working for his father's cloth business,' said Alice.

'I suppose it must. Anyway, shame on me, to be talking business to a bride on her wedding day!'

Alice smiled, nodded to him and his wife, and moved on. She was drawn to a dark-skinned woman with beautiful eyes, who wore a headscarf and stood beside a man who was in discussion with Henry.

'Alice, come here,' Henry called, smiling at her. She walked over, and he said, 'This is Mr. Farouk Mohamed, and his wife, Fatima.'

'Oh, you're Fatima!' said Alice.

The lady smiled at her and took Alice's hand. 'I have been looking forward very much to meeting you. I must say, you are every bit as lovely as your husband had led us to expect.'

Alice felt herself blush. 'Thank you – that's very kind.'

'I know you will be busy for a little while, setting up the house and so on, but I would be very happy to introduce you to the sights of Alexandria when you feel ready.'

'I would love that,' said Alice. 'I don't think there is very much to set up at the house. Henry took me to see it on the way here, and it all looks lovely.'

'Do you have mosquito nets in place?'

'Yes, and darling little shutters!'

Fatima smiled indulgently. 'These shutters are everywhere,' she said. 'But the mosquito nets, they are the most important item a house should have. I am pleased to hear you have them already installed.'

'Will the mosquitoes get very bad? I haven't been bitten so far.'

'They are always present, but they will come out in force next month, for the wet season.'

'Oh yes, the wet season,' said Alice. 'How wet will it be? Is it worse than England?'

'I have never had the good fortune to visit England. However, from other English people I have met here, I believe the rain will fall in much larger quantities, and in a much shorter space of time than you are used to.'

'Ah,' said Alice. 'Oh dear.'

Fatima laughed. 'We will plan some nice things to do indoors.'

Alice's father appeared at her elbow. 'So sorry to interrupt, but I believe it might be time to ask the guests to be seated for the wedding breakfast.'

'Oh, right!' said Alice. 'Please excuse me,' she said to Fatima.

'Of course. We shall have plenty of time to talk, once today is over.'

The rest of the day passed in a hum of conversation and a blur of faces. Alice's own face ached from smiling by the end of it. Finally, the last guest had said their farewells and she and Henry were able to bid her parents goodnight and head up to the suite her mother had reserved for their wedding night. Her parents were taking a taxi back to the San Stefano hotel, and they arranged to meet again soon after breakfast the following day.

In the lift, Alice leaned her head against Henry's chest and sighed with contentment.

'Happy?' he asked her.

'So, so happy.'

'This is the start of the rest of our lives together,' he said, bending to kiss her on the lips.

The doors opened and closed three times before the newlyweds stopped kissing for long enough to recall where they were. At last, they stepped out of the lift and in through the door of the honeymoon suite.

Chapter Twenty-Two

Thanks to Toby's evening ministrations, Miss Chevrolet started on the first attempt. Toby wound the crank handle and jumped in, just as the engine kicked into life.

'Here we go!' he called out, and the old car wended its way out of the garage. Fleur found the Chevy surprisingly easy to steer – but they made slow progress along the driveway, and then down the lane through the village. People stopped to watch their progress, and parents pointed out the car to their children, who ran excitedly alongside, waving to Fleur and Toby as if they were in a royal procession.

Fleur had put the roof back, and the air was sweet and warm on her face. She'd tied an ornate scarf she'd found in her grandmother's trunk over her hair, and was dressed in a lightweight driving coat and gloves, with large dark glasses.

'You look just the part for a drive in the country,' Toby had said, as he greeted her that morning with a kiss.

'So do you.' Toby had donned a tweed three-piece suit, with a cravat at the neck. She felt that they made quite a striking couple, as they proceeded at a sedate pace through the village, heading out to the country lanes beyond.

The scenery was like something from a Constable painting: brown cows grazing in fields beneath the wide spread of ancient oak trees. In many arable fields, the hay was drying in curious rolls, like the shells of gigantic garden snails.

'Shall we stop for a bit?' Toby said, after a while.

'Sure.' She parked Miss Chevrolet beside a farm gate a few yards further on. 'I'm not wearing my walking shoes.' She gestured to the slingback navy court shoes she'd unearthed that morning in her grandmother's collection.

'We don't need to go far. Hold on.' He reached into the back of the car and pulled out a hamper.

'Where did that come from?'

'I stashed it first thing this morning before you were up and about. I had to cover it with an old rug, so you wouldn't get suspicious.'

'What's in it?'

'Nice things to eat and drink. Just wait there a moment.'

He opened the gate into the field and carried through the hamper and the old rug. He spread the rug and walked back to the car, where he opened her door. Before she'd had time to anticipate his intention, he'd scooped her up and was carrying her into the field, where he laid her gently on the rug. Then he opened the hamper and unpacked freshly squeezed orange juice, a box of croissants and a thermos of hot chocolate.

'This is amazing,' she told him after they'd helped themselves. She was lying back, sipping at a mug of hot chocolate, in between taking bites from a still-warm croissant.

'I'm glad you like it. I went to the bakery the minute they opened this morning, and the croissants were fresh from their oven.'

'I feel as if I'm in France. We should be drinking our hot chocolate from breakfast bowls, instead of enamel mugs.'

'Mental note to self: next time, take Fleur to France,' said Toby.

'Ha! No, this is just fine. I love it.'

'You're a very special person, Fleur Cavendish,' said Toby.

'Thank you,' she said, with a blush. 'You're rather special yourself.'

The drive home after the picnic was even more lovely. They sat together in quiet contentment. Now and then, Toby pointed out a sight: a sparrowhawk in mid-chase; a hare racing across a field; or a deer, vanishing into a wood.

While they had been out on their jaunt, the dogs had been left to run amok in Toby's garden. Now, at the sound of the car's return to Wisteria Cottage, Hattie and Dougie arrived at the connecting gate, barking to be allowed access.

'I have to get back,' said Toby. 'I've got three bids to sift through, from builders in Manchester.'

'And I have initial sketches to produce for the V&A, plus more roughs for the butterflies' adventure book.'

'What a busy pair we are. Let's make sure we keep time in our busy lives for each other,' said Toby.

'I couldn't agree more,' said Fleur. 'It's going to be hard, though, if you're working in Manchester, and I'm travelling around.'

'We'll sort something out,' he said. He kissed her and headed over to the little gate. 'Dog coming through,' he called, as Hattie hurtled through the opened gate like a catapulted pea.

'Good girl,' called Fleur. 'Come and watch me work?'

She made a mug of tea and the two of them headed upstairs to the studio. This was so much a part of their routine now, that Fleur wondered if they would both miss it, after the move.

'And we still don't know where we're moving to,' she told Hattie. 'We must find somewhere soon.' She sighed and took out her pencils from their box as she seated herself at her desk with her sketchbook. Despite her imminent departure, something was stopping her from starting to look for a property – and she had more than a sneaking suspicion that that something was Toby.

Chapter Twenty-Three

1928

'Fatima has been so kind,' said Alice, over dinner. 'She took me to the local market today, and helped me to barter for vegetables.'

'You do know that we have servants to do that?' said Henry, smiling fondly at her as he sipped at his water.

'I know, but I want to experience everything about living here.'

'I see. So, what vegetables did you acquire?'

She looked sheepish. 'I don't know the names of half of them. I got some beautiful tomatoes, and something called an aubergine, which Fatima said would be nice in a *tagine*, whatever that is. Then there were some coloured capsicum – orange, and yellow, and green… I must admit, I was drawn more to the rich colours of the vegetables than to their practicality.'

He laughed. 'Let's hope Malik knows what to do with them all.'

'Oh, I'm sure he will. He is an excellent cook, isn't he?'

'Yes, I was very lucky. It was an expat couple who were moving back to the States, who passed him on to me. Fortunately, he seemed more than happy to come.'

'How do you order our food, Henry? I mean, how do you tell Malik what to cook?'

He laughed. 'I don't. I simply trust him to cook something good. My Arabic is still far from fluent, and I'm sure you've gathered that his English is non-existent.'

'Fatima's English is excellent.'

'Yes – I wonder why it's so good.'

'She told me today: apparently her school taught in English and French, so she is fluent in both of those, as well as Arabic.'

'That's amazing. It puts me to shame, with my few, stuttering words of Arabic.'

'We must try harder! It does seem to be the British way, to expect everyone else to speak our language.'

'You're right, my darling. I will get Freddie to teach me some more phrases.'

There was a pause, during which Alice put down her fork, in order to admire her husband: broad-shouldered and upright at the table; a kind expression on his handsome face.

He caught her eye. 'What is it?'

'I was just feeling proud to be married to you.'

'No, I'm the lucky one,' he said, smiling. 'So, what are your plans for tomorrow?'

'Oh, Fatima is going to take me to see some of the sights. Apparently, there are some lovely places to visit, just outside the town. She's going to take me in her car.'

'Fatima drives? Isn't that unusual here? I got the impression it was generally frowned upon.'

'What? For women to drive?'

'That's right.'

'I'm not sure that enough women own cars for the discussion to be warranted. Certainly, Fatima drives, although she is otherwise careful to obey social rules – in her dress, for instance. I find it astonishing, how narrow the women's rights seem to be, here: even narrower than in Britain.'

'Yes, it is a very traditional society. I sense that any social change will be slow. Are you going to be all right here?'

She laughed. 'Despite my lack of status? I think I can cope. It is much easier for me, with my liberal husband than for those women whose husbands treat them as inferior creatures.'

'But Fatima's husband, Farouk, is not like that, I trust?'

'Oh, no – Fatima says he is very generous and supportive.'

'Good. I had him down as a good man, and I would be sorry to have to alter that view.'

'Tell me about the sales division – how is it all progressing?'

'Pretty well, I think. We're rolling out new sales outlets in Cairo, Port Said and Luxor over the next six months or so. Sebastian Locksworth seems pleased with our progress. Meanwhile, Johnny Faraday back at Harpenden says the designers and engineers are working on the prototypes for "The Dash" and "The Curve".'

'That's wonderful news, darling – I'm so glad. And to think those new cars are all your idea!'

'It's funny, though…' he said.

'What is?'

'Well, before I met you, I'd have been over-the-moon to have success like this, so early on. Now, though, everything pales beside the need to be sure that you are happy.'

'As long as I'm with you, Henry, I can't imagine that I shall ever be unhappy.'

'I hope you always feel that way – you must promise to tell me if you ever feel less than happy here. Will you do that?'

'I will.'

'No, you must promise.'

'I promise,' she said, smiling at him.

'Very well,' he said. 'And now, let's find out what Malik has made for our dessert.'

***

Ten days later, the rains started. Alice gazed from the window, entranced by the drama of the season. Every leaf seemed painted a deeper green, glossy and fresh.

'How long will it last?' she asked Fatima, who had somehow made it over to the villa, to see her.

Her friend, standing beside her at the window, shrugged. 'This can vary. This month – October – is usually the worst, although there is a lot more rain in the winter than in the summer.'

Alice nodded. 'It is quite exhilarating, isn't it?'

Fatima smiled. 'This may not seem so exhilarating, once you have been trapped inside your house for many days.'

'Well, I suppose we won't be going for a walk!' said Alice.

'Not today, no. Nor, I suspect, for several weeks.'

'What would you like to do?' asked Alice.

A shy look came over Fatima's features. 'Would you show me some of your beautiful dresses?'

'With pleasure! I have some good hats, as well, which Mama designed for me. You know she runs a hat business?'

'I have heard this, yes. I am also very interested to see the hats.'

'Very well. I shall get them.'

'Won't your servants fetch them for you?'

Alice had been used to keeping servants in London; she had, however, been able to communicate with them. Here, she felt awkward, addressing the Egyptian servants in English, because her Arabic had not progressed beyond 'Salaam Alaikum', the traditional greeting. She found this phrase easy enough to remember because she had often heard Jewish friends of her parents greet one another with the curiously similar 'Shalom Aleichem'.

Henry, who had picked up a smattering of Arabic, kept assuring her that her lack of Arabic would not offend the servants. She found it hard, however, to get past the idea that she, as a visitor to their homeland, ought to be making more of an effort.

'Teach me Arabic,' she said on an impulse, turning to Fatima. 'Then I will be able to talk to people as I should.'

'This is not really necessary. Most educated people here speak English as well as Arabic and some also speak French and a local dialect. It is not unusual for people here to speak up to five languages.'

'Now I feel really ashamed,' said Alice, with a laugh.

'Everyone learns English: this is not your fault. You may as well benefit from it.'

Alice sighed. 'I suppose you are right. But it would help if you could teach me a few basics so that I do not feel the staff are bound to resent me.'

'Very well. We shall schedule a lesson for after the fashion display. This day will fly by!'

In the end, instead of bringing the clothes out to the living room, Alice took Fatima through to the bedroom, where she threw open the large mahogany wardrobes and Fatima gasped at the brocade, lace and embroidered gowns within.

'It is all so beautiful.'

'You are so pretty, you don't need finery,' said Alice. She was sincere: Fatima's fine, intelligent eyes shone from beneath her headscarf, lighting up her lovely face. Upon arrival, Fatima had removed the white scarf she wore over her face, hiding all but her eyes. The rest of her costume was black: a black gown, that covered her entire body.

'What do you want to see?' Alice asked. 'There are gowns that my mother had made especially for me, or the ready-made ones we picked up in the big stores in London. There are even a couple that were imported from Paris – a present from my uncle and aunt.'

'Oh, I would love to see those,' said Fatima.

'Very well. Take a seat, and I shall get them out for you.'

Fatima sat on a mahogany bedside chair, which had a velvet cushioned seat, while Alice pulled hangers from her wardrobes, laying dresses across the bed, for Fatima to admire.

The Parisian gowns were both day dresses in a fine white fabric, and each featured a drop waist and a sash. One dress bore a vivid orange embroidered flower on the left of the bodice, with a matching orange bow tied below the flower. The other featured a skirt of tiny pleats, with a large bow at the back of the dress. Both dresses were made from a rich silk, with a voile overlay.

'This orange flower is a Chinese influence,' said Alice. 'I'll show you my Chinese jacket, as well.' She drew the embroidered red coat from one of the wardrobes, and Fatima exclaimed at its loveliness.

Alice returned the Parisian frocks and the Chinese coat to her wardrobes, and then pulled out dresses in navy lace, and dancing gowns in organza.

After admiring many of the gowns, Fatima said:

'I have something to show you.'

'What?'

'Look...' Fatima lifted the bottom of her gown and revealed a beautiful petticoat, made from white lace and embroidered in gold.

'It's lovely,' said Alice. 'I had no idea...'

'I have to look unappealing to men other than my husband,' said Fatima. 'But I can wear nice things underneath, for both my own and his eyes alone.'

'And now mine,' said Alice.

They both laughed. 'But please don't speak of this to anyone,' said Fatima. 'It is private.'

'Of course, I won't,' said Alice. There was a pause. They listened to the rain beating hard on the roof of the little villa. 'I hope the house can cope,' she said.

'If not, it can be mended,' said Fatima. 'But houses here are built to take account of the rainy season. I am sure it will be fine.'

'So...tea?' suggested Alice.

'Tea would be lovely.'

She returned the remaining clothes to the wardrobes.

'These wardrobes are very fine,' said Fatima.

'Thank you. Henry chose the whole suite.'

'There are not many workmen who can create such intricate carvings,' said Fatima.

'I know: they are lovely, aren't they? I am lucky. Henry has such good taste.' The women admired the carvings of leaves and fruit, which framed the mirrors in the wardrobe doors. The bed had a matching headboard, and there were bedside cabinets in the same design. It was one of Alice's favourite rooms – filled with Henry, and with their shared love for beautiful things.

The women took tea in the living room, looking out on to the veranda – and the rain, which seemed relentless.

'When it's raining like this, I can't imagine it ever stopping,' said Fatima.

'That's just what I was thinking! Are you sure it will? What if it doesn't?'

Fatima laughed. 'I think the same thing every year, and every year it does stop. We just need to have faith. And, if not, we will have to build a boat!'

One of the servants brought a tray laden with tea things and set it on a table beside Alice.

'Thank you,' she said.

'Shukraan,' said Fatima quietly.

'Shu-ck-raan,' repeated Alice, committing the word to memory. The servant – a middle-aged woman, with a serious face, smiled and nodded, and Alice felt heartened. She would fit in here: it would simply require a little work on her part. After the servant left, Alice smiled at Fatima.

'What? What is it? Did I do something funny?'

Alice shook her head. 'No, I was just thinking that I am very lucky to have a friend like you.'

Fatima smiled. 'Ohhh, you know, I think we will both get much out of this friendship.'

***

Over the coming months, this prediction of Fatima's proved correct. Both women were delighted to have an intelligent, thoughtful companion, and their acquaintance deepened to a level at which they were relaxed and at ease together.

I do miss you, Suze, Alice wrote to her friend back home. *But at least, I have someone here – apart from Henry, of course – who understands me. I only wish I could introduce you and Fatima to one another... Write soon, and tell me of this Ferdinand, whom you mentioned in your last letter: is he still as wonderful as you thought? I hope so. I want you to be as happy as I, with my darling Henry.*

Chapter Twenty-Four

Fleur was in the kitchen, surrounded by trunks, boxes and packing cases when Toby walked in.

'Sorry,' he said. 'I did knock, but you didn't hear...'

She shook her head. 'No, that's fine. In fact, you're just in time to help me shut this packing case – the lid doesn't line up somehow.'

Toby walked over to the wooden crate and took a look. 'I think it's just because the tea tray is sticking up a bit on one side.' He gave the silver tray a nudge and it shifted into a better position. 'Let's try now.' They lined up the lid, and it slipped neatly into place.

'You're a star,' she told him.

'Hardly! I don't think managing to get a lid on to a box is a qualification for stardom.'

'On the day before I'm due to move house, it is, believe me.'

'So, what can I do to help?'

She looked at him, feeling gratitude well up with tears in her eyes. She blinked hastily.

'Would you bring down the suitcases that are in the back bedroom?' she asked.

'Of course – no problem.'

She wondered whether to tell him that there were a lot of suitcases – around fifty, at the last count. Then she decided to let him find out for himself: there was no reason to rush to impart bad news.

He left the room and she turned to the next packing crate. She had a large roll of bubble wrap, which she was using to pad and protect all of the china in the house. She sat down at the kitchen table, where she'd lined up the next tea set – a pretty, floral, Windsor set with a gold rim. She unrolled some bubble wrap and reached out for the first cup.

She heard Toby, overhead, enter the bedroom. Then she heard him exclaim. She smiled to herself as she wrapped cups and slotted them inside one another for protection en route to the storage facility, where most of her possessions would be held until she found a house of her own.

The stairs creaked as Toby came down, one suitcase in each hand. He placed them in the hallway, and then came into the kitchen.

'You didn't mention quite how many there were,' he said.

'Sorry...'

'I suppose, this is the sum of your grandmother's clothing collection.'

'And my mother's.'

'And yours?'

She shook her head. 'I haven't begun to pack my own clothes yet.'

'Look Fleur, I've been thinking...'

Not spotting his serious tone, she continued wrapping, simply saying, 'Uh-huh?'

He walked over to her and gently removed the cup from her hands.

'I need you to listen for a minute.'

She saw how earnest he was, and nodded.

'It just seems mad, you having to move away. Would you like to stay here?'

'If I could have afforded not to sell the house, I would definitely have kept it.'

He took a seat opposite her at the china-laden table.

'I've been thinking of a way for you to stay in the village.'

Meeting his eye suddenly became a problem. She found herself staring at Hattie, stretched out by the Aga as if the sleeping Labrador was fascinating.

'Fleur, look at me,' he said. She gingerly raised her blue eyes to meet his dark ones. 'I know it's early days for our relationship,' he continued, 'and I don't want to scare you off – but I think about you all the time. In fact, I can't stop thinking about you: the way you do the gardening in a silk tea dress with a 1970s' sunhat, and how you wear high heels to visit the mobile library. I love your art, and how creative you are – those pictures you draw, which seem to spool out from you, like a film of images you carry in your head.'

She stared at him in wonder, feeling happiness flood through her.

He carried on: 'I keep remembering how *at home* you looked in my house, when you waved to me from the window seat, on the night of the party. And I can't stop thinking about how kind you are, how thoughtful of others – or how unpleasant I was to you and poor Hattie, that first time we met, by the riverbank...'

'...She did spoil your smart work clothes.'

'Clothes can be cleaned,' he said, dismissively. 'Look at that wedding dress – it's as good as new, isn't it?' He had brought back the dress a few days earlier, and there had been no sign that it had ever borne the imprint of a toddler's hand. 'Fleur, what I'm trying to say is, would you consider moving in with me? I have plenty of storage space in the old barns, and I've already worked out that we could make you a studio in the second bedroom – it gets plenty of light and has those lovely views…'

Fleur could hold in her emotions no longer: she burst into tears.

'Hey…' Toby leapt to his feet and ran around to crouch beside her, where he put an arm around her and drew her against his chest. 'I didn't mean to make you cry. I'm so sorry.'

She shook her head, feeling the warmth of his chest through his shirt. She was aware that her tears were making a wet patch on the cotton fabric. 'It's not that. It's just…I think I'm in love with you.'

'In love? Really?' He pulled her away slightly, so he could see her face. 'Well, there's no need to cry about it!' Gently, he used his thumbs to wipe the tears from her cheeks, before taking a handkerchief from his pocket and handing it to her. She blotted her face and smiled ruefully at him.

'Sorry,' she said.

'What for? For finally telling me what I've been dying to hear?' He gazed down at her. 'You do know I've been in love with you for months, don't you? I felt ecstatic when we went for that walk in the woods, and you revealed you had feelings for me – I just wasn't sure how strong those feelings were.'

'Really?'

'Really.' He began his persuasive arguments again. 'And if you moved in, we could knock through into the box room, to create a walk-in wardrobe for you… And you could… '

'…It all sounds wonderful,' she said, interrupting him. 'Do you know what would make things even better?'

'What?' he asked, with genuine concern.

'If you could turn off your brilliant architect's brain and kiss me.'

Chapter Twenty-Five

1928-1930

The months passed, and Alice settled into her new life. The rains eased, and she was able to mingle with the other wives of the expatriate community in the area. Most of these women were friendly, and they compared their findings on Alexandrian society. It was considered inappropriate for a woman to walk alone, so they walked in a group if they walked at all. Sometimes, they visited the market, where Alice always found herself drawn to the brightly coloured spices and unfamiliar vegetables. With Fatima's help, she had picked up enough Arabic to barter and frequently amazed her companions by getting the prices down substantially.

With Fatima's support, Alice began to design hats again. The two women would debate styles and shapes, flicking through the Paris fashion magazines which Alice had arranged to have delivered.

'I like this shape,' Fatima would say, pointing to a ruched toque, or a cloche with an upturned brim.

'How about if we took that basic shape,' Alice would say, reaching for her sketchpad, 'but added a wave to the brim here, see?' She drew the rippled brim.

'I see. Yes, that would work – especially in a contrasting colour. Can your mother create that?'

'I don't know – we'll have to ask her and find out.'

The sketches would duly be sent off to London, whence, a month or so later, a prototype hat would arrive by mail. Whenever these boxes came, Alice waited for her friend before opening them. She would invite Fatima over for tea, and the two of them would sit, breath held, while one or other of them loosened the string on the package and removed the lid from the box. They would take it in turns to try on the hat and then inspect their reflection in a large hand mirror Alice kept in the living room especially.

One day, as they admired their reflections, Fatima said, 'These hats are lovely, but I can't wear them.'

'I know… It does seem a bit cruel – as if I'm taunting you with beautiful things you can't have. I did wonder if you might like to design some head scarves?'

Fatima smiled and drew a sheaf of papers from the bag at her feet. She held them out to Alice, who took them eagerly and rifled through them.

She looked up at her friend. 'How long have you been designing scarves?'

Fatima shrugged. 'Since I was small. I used to dream of wearing gorgeous, embroidered shawls and head scarves, but my mother said it wasn't…'

'…The done thing?' suggested Alice.

'Exactly.'

'She sounds just like my mother!'

'Really?' Fatima eyed Alice's knee-length lace dress doubtfully.

'Oh, I know I have far more freedom with my clothes than you, but don't you think we could create some of these?' She held up the sketches. 'Surely a little colour, or an embroidered edging, might be permissible?'

'I was thinking that Western ladies might like to wear them, to protect their hair while driving?'

'That's a great idea!'

'But how would we make them?'

'I'll ask my mother. I'll write today, and enclose some of your designs if I may? She's bound to be able to help – with advice, if nothing else.'

Alice's mother wrote back with enthusiasm, soliciting more of Fatima's sketches for scarves and shawls.

Fatima's designs grew more ambitious as time went by, and soon both ladies' names were associated with the designs for the 'Debonair Debutantes Collection': hats and scarves for the younger, more fashionable lady.

***

Occasionally, Henry invited Alice into the office. He would lead her around the storage depot, pointing out the various car parts that represented innovations in the motoring world – whilst all the while proudly showing off his pretty wife. She, for her part, would pretend not to notice.

She loved seeing him at his work. He was clearly popular with his workers, and she felt proud of his fairness as a manager.

Once, he had come home upset: a boy had hurt himself, carrying too many crates at once.

'I tell them, over and over, not to take more than one crate at a time,' he told her, as they ate dinner.

'Is he badly injured?'

'Quite badly. The crates crushed his right foot. The doctor thinks he might still keep his foot, thank goodness, but he will almost certainly have to walk with a stick. The trouble is, he is his family's main breadwinner.'

'How old is he?'

'Sixteen – but a silly, immature sixteen. Freddie only employed him, because he took pity on the boy's family.'

'And now what will happen?'

'We have a sickness fund set up, but it won't be enough to keep his mother and three sisters fed and clothed.'

'Do his sisters work?'

'I think they take in sewing work.'

'I wonder if they could be useful for a new project Fatima and I are planning.'

'You're a dark horse, aren't you? What is this project?'

'We were thinking we might be able to manufacture some hats and head scarves, on a small basis, here in Alexandria. As you know, there's quite a big expatriate community and a lot of the women seem genuinely interested in the prospect of buying fashionable headgear locally. We might also be able to appeal to some of the Egyptian women, with the scarves.'

'That sounds like a great idea. I may even know of a workspace that might suit you.'

The next evening, he escorted Fatima and Alice to a small factory unit within a much larger building. They walked through other units on the way – past dressmakers and dyers, knitters and weavers.

'You see, it's all cottage industries here,' he said. 'Small-scale businesses.' They came to the empty unit, and he unlocked the door and showed them inside. 'What do you think?'

It was a large, white-painted room, with a wooden floor and big windows, through which light streamed.

'I think it's perfect,' said Fatima. 'What do you think, Alice?'

'I agree. How much is it to rent?'

The rent was surprisingly affordable, and the two women were able to set up their factory the following week, having borrowed sewing machines from everyone they could approach. They found a cloth maker in the building, who was happy to supply bolts of thick felts and woollen cloth to the ladies for the hats. Fatima toured the Alexandrian cloth factories for finer silks for her scarf line.

The two ladies' first hiring was the three sisters of the wounded boy: two as machinists, and the third as a materials cutter. These three women proved excellent workers, and Fatima and Alice soon stopped examining their seams or cutting lines, knowing they could trust them to produce high-quality work.

Fatima also found a grandmother and granddaughter team who possessed excellent embroidery skills – the girl had learnt from her grandmother. Fatima hired them at once, and these two women set to work, interpreting their employer's sketches into needlework, in the form of elegant scrolls or striking florals.

'I was thinking that we could also feature this embroidery on some of the hats,' said Fatima, a week after the company launched its operations.

'What a wonderful idea!' said Alice. 'Some of the Western women might like to buy a set, of a hat and matching scarf.'

'Exactly.'

Within just two weeks, the first hats and scarves were on display in a local boutique. These prototypes sold the same day, and orders came flooding in. The factory expanded its production, taking in more workers. Alice's Arabic improved, as she relaxed into her role as joint-manager and -business owner of this millinery and scarf business, which they named 'Alisma' – being a combination of *Alice* and *Fatima*.

Alice wrote to her mother with queries about shaping felt, or with difficulties in creating a particular type of brim from stiffened organza, and her mother wrote back, including diagrams and cutting patterns, which helped to resolve these issues.

Soon, Fatima and Alice were designing almost full-time, chatting and laughing as they played around with fabric. Fatima would go through the Paris fashion journals as soon as they came in, making a note of the hat shapes she felt would suit the Alisma market, and sketching ideas for scarves that might be paired with them, for women who wanted to buy a matching set. Then she and Alice would sit down together, to work out how these styles could be altered and enhanced. Every Alisma hat-and-scarf set was a joint product, the result of these two women working together, with the same aim: to create wearable items that were, nonetheless, works of art.

***

After the darkness of winter, Alice and Henry made the most of the lighter evenings that arrived in the spring, by taking an after-dinner, arm-in-arm walk together.

'I do so love being here with you,' he would tell her.

'And I, with you.'

One evening, he told her: 'I spend all day thinking of how I will see you again when I get home.'

She laughed. 'I hope you concentrate a little more than that on your work.'

'Oh, just enough,' he said. 'How's your own work going?'

'Pretty well.' She moved to stand in front of him. 'There is one thing I've been wanting to talk to you about…'

'Is everything all right?' he asked, with concern.

'I'm fine – if you discount the sickness in the mornings after you've gone off to work.'

'Sickness?' She watched his face move from anxious to excited.

'You mean…?'

'I'm pregnant, darling – we're going to have a baby!'

'Oh, Alice!' He hugged her tightly, and then released her, saying, 'Is that all right? I won't damage the baby, will I?'

She laughed. 'No, I think the baby will like to know its parents love one another.'

'Shouldn't you be sitting down?'

She shook her head 'There will be time enough for sitting when I can't see my feet. Let's walk for now.'

After the initial morning sickness, Alice kept well and was able to continue working with Fatima. One day, as they were sitting together at their design desks in a corner of the factory, Alice said,

'I'm going to miss you, Fatima.'

'And I, you, Alice Pemberton.'

'I have made something for you. I hope it's all right…' She produced a package from beneath the desk and passed it to her friend. Fatima took it and said,

'What is this?'

'It's my going-away present to you. Open it.'

Fatima untied the bow and unfolded the delicate tissue paper. Inside the parcel, there was a black, frilled petticoat in black, with flowers embroidered on it in red and gold, among green leaves.

'Oh! It's beautiful!' she exclaimed. 'But how did you…?'

'Oh, Sahirah and her grandmother worked it for me, secretly – I copied the design from your book of Spanish embroidery.'

'It is so lovely… I think Farouk will like this, too.' She got up to hug Alice. 'Thank you,' she said. 'It shall remind me of you. I wish you weren't going.'

'I know,' said Alice 'I feel torn. I want to be among family, but this is so hard…'

'Write to me,' said Fatima.

'Of course – so long as you write back.'

'I shall: I promise.'

***

'You're coming home?' Alice's mother's voice was distorted by distance down the phone line, but her excitement came through clearly.

'There is a reason, Mummy,' said Alice.

'Oh no – it's not Henry's job, is it?'

'No, Mummy. Guess again.'

'You're not… Oh, Alice! Are you pregnant?'

'Six months now. I want to have the baby back home, and then we're going to stay in England – permanently, I mean.'

'Oh, darling, how exciting!' Her voice retreated even further through the fog of miles as she called to Alice's father: 'Thomas! Thomas! Come here! Alice is having a baby!'

Her father's voice came on the line. 'Alice, is it true? Am I going to be a grandfather?'

'It's true, Daddy.'

'Oh, darling, that's wonderful. But are you going to have the baby in Egypt?'

'No, I'm coming home. I'm leaving next week.'

It was her father's turn to take his mouth from the receiver: 'She's coming home, Christine!'

'I know – isn't it exciting? Now, let me have the telephone back.'

Her mother's voice came back on the line. 'What do you need, darling?'

'Nothing. Henry's going to come back with me. They've fixed up a job for him at Luton.'

'Not a demotion, I hope?'

'Oh no, nothing like that. In fact, he's going to a more senior role, as head of new product development. Since GM bought out Harpenden, Henry's designs – you know, "The Curve" and "The Dash" – have been such a great success, that they're dying to have him back at head office.'

'I can't believe you're coming back,' said her mother. 'I'll have to tell everyone – they'll all want to see you.'

'Don't forget I'm pregnant,' said Alice. 'I don't have as much energy as before.'

'Of course,' said her mother, 'I wasn't thinking. I'll wait until you're back and then we can see how you're feeling. You're keeping well, though?' her voice sounded anxious.

'Very well, Mummy – apart from the usual morning sickness near the start.'

'I can't believe you kept it from us for all these months.'

'I wanted to be sure it was all progressing properly before I told anyone back home. Not that I've been able to hide it from anyone here, of course – my stomach's enormous.'

Her father came back on the line. 'What about the car?' he asked.

'What do you mean?'

'Well, are you leaving it behind?'

'No, GM are shipping Miss Chevrolet home for us, so we'll still have her. Not that she's our main car, these days – Henry has to drive one of the latest models, as he's representing the firm.'

'Of course – I hadn't thought of that. That Chevy's part of your history, though, isn't it? Something to show your children.'

Alice smiled at how her father seemed more interested in Miss Chevrolet than in the imminent arrival of his first grandchild.

'I have to go now, Daddy. Some of the girls are coming round.'

'All right, darling. Lots of love and congratulations to you and Henry from both of us. We'll look forward to seeing you soon.'

'See you soon, Daddy.' Alice put down the receiver and rubbed her sore belly button. The baby was kicking hard, but then, it never seemed to stop – a sure sign it was a boy, according to the midwife. Fatima had pooh-poohed this idea:

'This is nonsense, Alice. My sister's daughter, Maya, kicked far harder than her brothers. It simply means that you are carrying a strong, healthy child – though it possibly has quite a stubborn nature.'

'Oh, dear.'

Fatima had smiled at her. 'Yes, you may need to be prepared to be a strict mama at times, or that child will run rings around such an easy-going lady as you.' She paused, then asked, 'Are you glad to be going home, to your parents?'

'Oh, yes: it will be lovely to live near them again.'

'You will not live in their house?'

Alice shuddered. 'No – General Motors is finding us a small house until we can find something to buy. I think it might be a bit much for Mummy and Daddy, to have a whole family, including a new baby, living with them.'

'It is true that I sometimes wish that we didn't have to live with Farouk's father. His mother is wonderful: very helpful and kind. However, his father does nothing but sit, all day long, and demand that we fetch him tea and tobacco.'

'He is an old man, though, isn't he?'

'Yes, he is eighty-three. It is not really his fault: he complains that his legs don't work like they used to.'

'That must be hard for him. I don't envy you, living with your in-laws, though. I think Henry feels he has had a narrow escape, thanks to the firm's owning this house, near the plant in Luton.'

Fatima took Alice's hand. 'I will miss you,' she told her.

Alice held out her arms and the two women hugged. 'I will miss you, too, Fatima – so very much. You have been my friend and made me feel at home in a new country, where I was afraid I might be entirely alone, except for Henry.'

'You would never be alone,' said Fatima, in decided tones. 'You are one of those rare people who draw others to themselves, wherever they are.' They smiled at one another.

Then Fatima said, 'I have a little secret myself: I am also pregnant.'

'Fatima! That's wonderful news!' Alice felt suddenly sad. 'We will not know each other's children,' she said.

'We will write about them in our letters,' said Fatima. 'It will be as though we are seeing them ourselves.'

'What about the factory?'

'Oh, I think we could promote those sisters,' said Fatima. 'What do you think?'

Alice thought about the three women they had employed as the first workers at the Alisma millinery factory. 'That's an excellent idea. We can give them a big pay rise, too – we can afford it, now. Thaminah has shown a real aptitude for the design side, so she can take over there.'

The Alisma millinery business had been so successful, that she and Fatima had been obliged to move it to larger premises. Now, it took up an entire, two-storey building in the industrial area, and even incorporated its own shop, selling directly to its fashion-hungry customers.

Alice felt relieved to know that the business would continue, albeit without the direct involvement of either of its founders.

'I must get back,' said Fatima. 'My father-in-law will be crying out for his lunch.'

They shared another hug, and then Alice waved to Fatima, who headed back to her car. Alice continued to wave as Fatima drove away down the bumpy track. The sun was hot, and Alice walked gratefully into the shade of the veranda. The baby was kicking hard, so she sank into the swing seat, where she found the baby was always calmed by its gentle, swinging motion.

They were to leave the next day, and Henry had gone to the office only to finish passing on instructions and information to the new man, who had arrived two weeks earlier.

Soon, they would be back in England. She would miss this house and the near-constant sunshine. She would miss her friend Fatima, and many of her other friends here in Alexandria.

She would not, however, miss the rainy season – or the way the access track to the villa was prone to flooding and becoming impassable.

She would miss the beautiful views, but not as much as she missed hearing English spoken all around her. She had begun to dream in Arabic, and she was afraid she might lose her identity if she stayed much longer.

The baby had quietened, so she wandered into the house, where packing cases stood all around the rooms, some nailed shut, and others gaping open, waiting to be fed with more household items.

Yes, she thought: it was time for Henry and herself to move on to a new stage in their lives.

Epilogue

'How's it going?' Toby had appeared in the doorway of the studio, bearing a mug of tea and a plate of chocolate digestives.

'Take a look.'

He put down the mug and plate, and then walked around to her side of the desk, where he peered over her shoulder at the fashion sketches she was working on.

'Those look great – nineteen-twenties, am I right?'

'Quite right: drop waists, rosettes, ribbons, bows, fringes, pointed shoes, cloches, toques…'

'Don't you own all of those?'

'Most of them,' she admitted, with a laugh. 'Although I am thinking of asking the V&A if they'd be interested in some of the more iconic pieces.'

'You mean you'd be willing to give away some of your grandmother's clothing?'

'Only to the V&A – I have to be sure it will be taken care of by experts. Some of the pieces from later decades are by Vivienne Westwood, Mary Quant, Chanel…'

'You can't give away the Mary Quant – you love those dresses.'

'True. I might hold on to those.'

'So…did you hear yet from Bloomsbury, about whether they like the butterflies book?'

'Not yet. I'm trying not to check my emails compulsively. My agent says she'll let me know, as soon as she hears anything.'

He laughed. 'I'm sure you'll hear soon. Those so-called "roughs" you did looked pretty complete to me – and they were beautiful.'

'Have you had any news from the builders in Manchester?' she asked him.

'Not today, but that's generally a good sign – they tend to call only when they've hit a snag. I thought we might have a weekend up there next week, though, if you fancied it? We could visit the Whitworth Art Gallery, which I think you'd love. It's full of Andy Warhol screen prints, Henry Moore sculptures and fantastic fifties' mobiles in those geometric shapes.'

'That sounds great. You book it, and I'll definitely come along!'

He put his arms around her, and she leant back against him.

'Happy?' he asked her.

'So happy,' she said. 'I am surrounded by beautiful things, and I live with a handsome man in a gorgeous, converted mill…'

'No regrets, then?'

She gazed out of the window, to where Miss Chevrolet was just a shape, hiding beneath her cover in the open garage.

'None whatsoever,' she told him.

***

1978

Alice and Henry stood and waved to their grandchildren as their daughter's car headed away down the driveway. They could just make out Fleur's little hand still waving, as the car disappeared around the curve.

'Well, it's certainly going to be quiet around here now,' said Henry, with a laugh. He kissed the top of his wife's head. 'Fancy a stroll?'

They walked slowly, arm in arm, through the garden. The sun was low in the sky, dipping everything in golden light. When they reached the furthest reaches of the garden, they turned to look at the house.

'I love it here,' said Alice, marvelling at the way the old redbrick farmhouse shone like a torch in the gloaming.

'Me, too,' said Henry. 'I tell you what: shall we pay Miss Chevrolet a visit before we go in?'

'Yes, let's.'

They walked over to the stable-style building in which the old car was garaged. Inside, Henry removed the cover and opened the passenger's door, and Alice climbed in. This was no longer the simple act it had once been – her joints were not as smooth on their hinges as they had once been.

Once his wife was safely inside, Henry closed the door and walked around to the driver's side. He climbed in and closed his own door.

'Where to, Ma'am?' he asked her, and she laughed.

'Hmm. The seaside, perhaps. I'd like to take a tour of the South-west coast.'

Henry saluted smartly as if his trilby hat were really a chauffeur's cap.

'Very well, Ma'am.'

He pretended to drive for a moment or two, and then he let his hands drop softly from the steering wheel, and they gazed out through the open doorway of the garage, into the soft evening light.

'I feel so happy, just sitting here with you,' Alice told him.

'It's perfect, isn't it?' said Henry. 'I could sit here forever.'

'But you might get hungry,' pointed out Alice.

'Ever-practical,' said Henry, but he said it with affection. He leaned over and kissed the top of her head. Her hair had turned a beautiful, pure white with age. She wore it in a neat knot at the nape of her slender neck. She still held herself as upright as in her youth, and she had never lost her style and poise. That day, she was dressed in a teal-coloured, knee-length dress with a full skirt, which she'd cinched in at the waist with a wide belt. The dress had a matching bolero jacket. The dark blue-green brought out the green of her lovely eyes.

Before they left the garage, Henry tucked Miss Chevrolet safely back beneath her blanket, for another long sleep.

Then he put an arm around his wife's shoulders, and the two of them walked out and stood, gazing at the house in which they had raised their children – and in which their beloved grandchildren now regularly romped.

'This is all I ask,' said Henry, 'to grow even older here, with you, in this lovely place.'

He bent to kiss his wife, and she put her arms around him. They stood there, quietly content in each other's embrace until the night had wiped out all traces of the sun, and the stars shone down, like millions of blessings, on their love.

si on est amoureux, il n'y a pas besoin de la lune.*

---

* If there is love, there is no need of the moon

Philippa Church has a new range of greetings cards. The designs are hand painted watercolours, by Philippa and lovingly reproduced as a signed print onto 135mm x 135mm (5.25" x 5.25") folded card (with matching envelope).

The cards will be distributed under the name of Garden Flowers Cards and each design has been inspired by flowers in the gardens where Philippa received so much inspiration and enjoyed so much happiness.

The range is extensive and Philippa will be delighted to send her complete listing of cards for your attention.

Enquiries.gardenflowerscards@gmail.com

Lightning Source UK Ltd.
Milton Keynes UK
UKOW06f1113070916

282401UK00009B/46/P